D1190823

Adventures in Nature

*Stories, Activities
and Inspiration for
all the Family*

DAWN NELSON

The
History
Press

First published 2021

The History Press
97 St George's Place, Cheltenham,
Gloucestershire, GL50 3QB
www.thehistorypress.co.uk
© Dawn Nelson, 2021

British Library Cataloguing in Publication Data.
A catalogue record for this book is available from the British Library.

ISBN 978 0 7509 9510 8

Typesetting and origination by Typo•glyphix
Printed in Great Britain by TJ Books Ltd

MIX
Paper from
responsible sources
FSC® C013056

Contents

Acknowledgements

This book would not have been possible without many people. Audiences who have listened to my stories, the patrons who support my work via Patreon, my daughter who has, by insisting I tell certain stories over and over, shown me which ones sing to people's hearts and, of course, my husband, who has supported me in so many ways throughout the writing of this book.

These stories came about when I challenged myself to write 100 mini fables in 100 days. What appeared on the pages were tiny glimpses of childhood stories that have stayed with me and have woven themselves into my own tales; narratives inspired by sunshine-filled days in the country, learning about nature, and time spent listening to my mother read at bedtime, and so for that I am forever grateful to my mother for her love of nature and literature and for passing that on to me.

My thanks also to Nicola Guy at The History Press for seeing the potential in this book and to the rest of the team for working so hard to bring it into being.

Introduction

Merry met, reader of tales and adventurer of life. My name is Dawn Nelson, and I am an author and professional storyteller. As a teller I am known as DD Storyteller and I love to tell both traditional tales and my own original stories, which often combine folklore, nature and the old ways.

In this book, you will find a collection of original, seasonal stories that hold within them elements of nature and echoes of our ancestors' stories. The book is divided into the twelve months of the year and there are four stories for each month.

The stories use nature to teach us something about ourselves and how we connect with the world around us. Each story also has an activity to accompany it. After you have read one of the stories for the month that we are currently in, you can then turn to that month's activities section and there you will find an adventure, craft project or recipe that will help you to bring the story to life with the younger members of your family. You are also encouraged to keep an Adventure Journal, with notes of your finds and discoveries while carrying out these activities.

At the back of the book is a list of resources for each month's activities. These are websites and books that you can use to find more information to help you with the activity, should you wish.

Within the book there is also a chance to pause for the wheel of the year as it turns and learn about the ancient festivals of Imbolc, Ostara, Beltane, Litha, Lammas, Mabon, Samhain and Yule.

This collection contains forty-eight stories for families. They encompass my love for fable, folklore and fairy tale and, as you read, you may discover echoes of past stories told to you and themes running through them that are present in many of the long-told tales of our ancestors. Like a magpie takes shiny items for their nest, so a storyteller weaves old stories into new.

Stories are in our blood, stitched into the fabric of our being, the very essence of what it is to be human. They help us to learn, to explain the world around us and to perpetuate our cultures and beliefs. Holding many of them dear, we hand stories down through the generations as keys to our own hopes and fears, and I hope that these stories will, in turn, be passed on to the next generation so that they will also tell them.

January

Bare trees in the winter dark
Badgers slumber, foxes bark
Catkins dance from branches high
Listen, the sleeping earth it sighs.

The Old Oak Tree

Journey through the valleys and across the hills, and you will reach a forest full of oak trees. They have been standing there for as long as the Earth has been turning. Each year new trees are born, and old ones fall back to the earth. It's the cycle of the forest, but to truly see the magic, you must look a little closer.

The huge oak tree that once stood at the centre of the forest is now just a stump. It started its life as an acorn, burying itself deep into the leaf mulch to find a warm bed. As the weather grew cold, the acorn dug further down and was covered by more leaves and twigs. Feathers and fur from the passing animals fell too, to warm the acorn. The acorn stayed very still and waited.

Spring came and the birds shouted from the trees: 'The sun is here once more!'

The acorn heard their call and stretched. As it did, its shell cracked, and a small, green shoot emerged. Each day, the sun shone a little more and the shoot pushed through the soil. Poking through the leaves it saw the forest around it, towering above.

Rain arrived and the little shoot drank, thirsty from its efforts. It grew and grew and grew, and as it got bigger more animals began to visit it.

First came the ants, hurrying up and down the shoot to collect its old leaves as they shrivelled; next the beetle, who was looking for a place to shelter from the rain. The shoot grew stronger, and soon birds were able to perch on it to look for worms on the forest floor. Its trunk got stouter, and it grew taller still until, eventually, the birds could nest in its branches.

Bigger and bigger, higher and higher the oak tree reached. Over the years it had many animals make it their home: barn owls, woodpeckers, squirrels, woodlice, beetles, butterflies and gall wasps. The tree helped them all.

Fifty years the tree was standing, growing strong, basking in the warmth of the sun's rays and soaking up the rain of many clouds. Then a terrible storm came. From a heavy grey sky, the wind howled, and thunder rumbled right down to the roots of the tree. A twist of fate, a misplaced branch, and the tree was struck by lightning. It split in two.

The next day, a woodcutter travelling through the forest saw that the tree had been damaged by the storm. They saw that it could not grow anymore and that it may fall and take other trees with it; other trees that were not yet ready to meet the earth. And so, the woodcutter set to work. They cut the dead branches of the tree away until all that was left was the stump. They took the wood home to make a fire to warm their house and cook food for their family.

They did not take more than they needed, though. They knew the tree had helped someone else, but it was not done yet. In fact, it's still there in the forest.

If you look at the bottom of the old oak stump you can see a beetle has made its home among the leaves. A little mouse lives in a hollow of the root and mushrooms grow from the bark. If you look really, really closely, you can see the shoots of an acorn that fell the day the tree was struck by lightning. It is growing strong and reaching high.

The oak tree will grow again and help many more animals of the forest. So next time you see an oak tree, remember its journey. That is the magic of the forest.

Who's Afraid of the Big Bad Wolf?

Did you know there is a wolf in your garden? Don't worry, it's not a big howling, furry grey wolf. It's a tiny wolf spider. Come with me; let's have a look.

Between the cracks in the wall that run around the back of my garden, there is the most magnificent spider's web. It may be small, but its strands of thread are strong and tough, and the web is known throughout the garden as a place from which none can escape. It has been spun by the wolf spider, a hairy black beast that lurks in the crevice of the wall and rushes at any insect that may stray too close to his home.

One day, a little ladybird was passing the wolf spider's house. She was on her way up the wall to visit the woodlouse family. One of the little woodlice had been ill for some time and so the ladybird had made some of her medicinal elderberry rob cordial and was taking it to the mother woodlouse.

As she passed the crack in the wall, where the wolf spider lived, he rushed out to grab her.

'Stop!' said the little ladybird. 'I have important supplies to deliver.'

For some reason, this time the wolf spider did stop. Perhaps it was curiosity, or the unusual bravery of such a little bug that made him hesitate.

'Where are you going?' he asked. 'What is so important that I should forgo my lunch?'

'The smallest woodlouse is very sick, and I must hurry to get him his medicine by dinner time.'

'You have plenty of time,' the spider said, looking up at the sun. 'It is only one o' clock, but of course, you must be on your way.' He gave the ladybird a large hairy grin from leg to leg as she hurried on by.

The ladybird couldn't believe her luck as she scurried on up the wall. What she didn't realise was that the wolf spider knew of the woodlice in the garden but did not know where to find their home. Now he did. And now he knew where to get a free meal.

Running on up the wall, under the cover of the ivy, he overtook the ladybird and arrived at the woodlouse's house. He ransacked the little nest, sending the woodlice to all the corners of the wall. Those who did not run fast enough made a tasty lunch for the wolf spider. He licked his lips and settled into the little woodlouse's bed to await the arrival of the ladybird.

'Hello,' came the voice of the ladybird but she received no reply.

Full of woodlice, the wolf spider had fallen asleep; his belly round and wriggling with the tiny creatures. The ladybird got quite a shock when she saw the writhing stomach of the wolf spider and heard tiny voices from within. You see, in his hurry to eat all the woodlice the wolf spider had swallowed them alive.

Being careful not to wake the wolf spider, the little ladybird took a thorn from a nearby bramble and cautiously opened his stomach to set the woodlice free. Then she carefully sewed the wolf spider's stomach back up with one of his own silken threads. All the while, the spider was asleep. The ladybird and the woodlice disappeared back into the ivy and left the wolf spider snoring loudly.

When he awoke, he found the house empty and a terrible itching in his stomach. For, when the ladybird had stitched him back up, she had filled his tummy with nettles! From that day on, the wolf spider stayed away from the woodlice and the ladybird now lives in happy peace beside the log pile.

It's safe to say that the wolf spider has learnt his lesson but, then again, so has the little ladybird.

Pulling it out of the Hat

Once upon a time, there was a little boy, called Sebastian, who so wanted to be a magician. He practised every moment of every day and every night, but he still couldn't master the most basic trick – pulling a rabbit out of a hat. He tried every which way to say the spell and, no matter how many times he tried, nothing happened; not even a scrap of fur appeared; not even a fluffy tail, a twitchy nose or a pair of pointy ears.

He practised everywhere he could – meadows, forests, park benches – and one day, when he was on his way home, he saw a poster announcing the arrival of the Grand Magi in his town. He knew this was his chance and so he bought himself a ticket for the next evening's performance.

The evening came, and on entering the tent he found there were rows and rows of people standing to watch already and he couldn't see a thing. He heard the oohs and the aahs as the Grand Magi performed trick after trick. There was one final, tremendous round of applause and the show was all over. Sebastian hadn't seen any of it. Feeling downhearted, he left.

As he walked around the back of the tent to go home, he spotted light from under it and could see feet moving around. He heard the voice of the Grand Magi. He just had to get in there to talk to him. Squeezing under the edge of the tent, Sebastian arrived in the dressing room of the Grand Magi. Hands on hips, the Grand Magi's assistant demanded to know what Sebastian thought he was doing.

'It's obvious isn't it?' said the Grand Magi. 'He wants to see me and ask me about one of my tricks. Let him in and give him a glass of water, for goodness' sake, he looks most flustered.'

'Th-Thank you,' stuttered Sebastian, taking the water from the assistant and gulping it. It had been hot in the tent and Sebastian's mouth was suddenly very dry.

'So, which trick do you wish to learn, boy?' the Grand Magi asked.

'I would love to know how to pull a rabbit out of a hat,' said Sebastian. 'I have practised and practised but still I have not mastered it.'

'That's an easy one, if you know how, of course,' said the Grand Magi, stroking his beard. 'First of all, you need to think like a rabbit: What does he eat? What does he look like? What does he do all day?'

It all sounded very strange to Sebastian and he went to say something, but the Grand Magi raised a finger to stop him.

'Finally, and this is the most important ingredient, you need a drop of perspiration.'

'What's that?' asked Sebastian, for he had never heard of perspiration.

'Something you only get when you have been working very hard. Now, off you go and don't break into my tent again.'

Sebastian left in a hurry, thanking the Grand Magi once more. On the path home, he stopped to sit on a fallen log, to ponder what the Grand Magi had said.

He looked up at the clear night sky and talked himself through the Grand Magi's instructions.

'Think like a rabbit? Hmm … let's start with an easier one. What does a rabbit eat? Carrots and grass of course! What does he look like? White with a cotton wool tail! What does he do all day? He hops around and spends his time alert and vigilant. I've got it!'

Sebastian shot off the log and ran all the way home. Grabbing his magician's hat, he collected carrots from the kitchen, cotton wool from his mother's medicine chest and grass from the garden, before running to the bottom of his garden and putting the items into the hat. Then he hopped up and down holding the hat and saying the magic words. He thought hard about being a rabbit and listened to all the noises of the night around him: the screech of an owl, the rustle of a mouse and the crack of the tree branches up above. He hopped until the sun was coming up and he could feel the sweat beading on his forehead – but still there was no rabbit.

Looking down into the hat, he sighed, muttering the spell one last time. As he did, a drop of sweat rolled off his forehead and landed in the hat. Kaboom! A puff of smoke and a big, white, fluffy rabbit appeared. At last Sebastian had performed his first magic trick!

So, you see, with a little thought, some hard work and a drop of perspiration, you'll always pull it out of the hat!

The Village Cauldron

It had been a hard winter in the village of Esuriit. Everyone was hungry. The farmer was down to her last few beans, the baker, the last of his oats and the cottage gardeners, their last few vegetables. There was little left for anyone and so a village meeting was called to decide what they should do about it. They desperately needed good weather to help the crops.

'I have no chickens left,' Rose, the farmer, complained. 'Only bones and they will make no one a meal.'

'I can't make bread anymore,' shrugged the baker. 'I'm not sure what we're all supposed to do?'

'We could walk to the next village,' suggested Lily, the granddaughter of the village's wise woman.

'I've heard they have nothing either,' said the vicar.

'Then we should gather together our resources,' said Lily.

'We have no resources! Haven't you been listening? There is nothing left,' the villagers exclaimed.

'Ah, but we do!' Lily turned to the blacksmith. 'If you can get a fire going in the middle of the village, I shall bring the large cast iron cauldron I have from my grandmother's time. You …' Lily pointed at the villagers as she spoke, 'you must bring what you have: chicken bones, beans, oats, the last of the carrots – whatever it is, please bring it.'

Lily, only slight of frame and even thinner from hunger, dragged the cauldron to the centre of the village. As she did so, her grandmother's voice rang in her ears: 'Keep the cauldron well and it will serve you … but never tell its secret for the villagers will not trust you.'

Lily had done just this. She had kept it safe, kept it clean and kept it from rusting and had never told its secret. Now, when the village was desperate, it was time to see what the cauldron could do.

As soon as she got to the middle of the village, where the blacksmith had made the fire, she asked him to make a stand on which to put the cauldron. She filled the cauldron with water from the well and placed it on the stand above the fire. As the villagers arrived, she got them to put the things they had brought into the cauldron.

The pot began to boil and, as more and more villagers placed their leftovers in it, tendrils of aromatic steam rose from it. Tummies rumbled and lips were licked. The villagers could now see what Lily had in mind.

'The Grand Soup is ready!' Lily announced, and the villagers queued with their bowls as Lily ladled it out. 'What is a little for one, together is plenty for all!'

'Hear, hear!' the villagers cheered, as their bellies were full. For the next few weeks, the blacksmith kept the fire going and the cauldron was replenished with whatever the villagers found at the back of their pantries. The cauldron served them well.

None of them could explain why, no matter what the ingredients, the soup always tasted delicious. But they didn't care. The Grand Soup got them through the tough times.

Soon the rain fell, the sun shone, and the crops grew again. Spring was here. The fire was extinguished beneath the cauldron and Lily put the cauldron away again until the villagers might have need of it once more. Only Lily knew the truth. She could still see the twinkle in her grandmother's eye.

'Keep the cauldron well and it will serve you … but never tell its secret: it's magic.'

Activities

Starting your Adventure Journal

Throughout this book, you will find a variety of different adventures to go on, just like the characters in the stories. These adventures will also help you to create your very own stories, so now is a great time to start your 'Adventure Journal'.

You can use a notebook, but if you'd like to make your own, why not take some scrap paper, punch some holes on one edge and lace it together with string, wool or thread. Write, draw and even stick things in that you find on your adventures. Just remember that there are a few rules for adventuring:

* Always make sure you are wearing the correct clothing and footwear so that you will be warm and dry.
* Always take an adult with you.
* Stick to the footpaths.
* Make sure you ask an adult before you pick anything or take anything home.
* Leave nothing behind. Take all your belongings and rubbish home with you.

Old Tree Stump Finds

For this month's adventure, we are going into the wood to see if we can find an old tree stump, like the one in the story of 'The Old Oak Tree'. For this adventure, you might want to take with you:

* a finds tub – these are usually small, round containers with a magnifying glass on the top
* your Adventure Journal
* a pencil
* binoculars
* a snack and a drink for refuelling.

The next job is to find an old tree stump. If you don't have any woodland near you then you could try looking for where shrubs have been cut back in the local park.

Once you have found your habitat, take a look around it, under the leaves, broken twigs and old seed heads, and see if you can find any insects. You may find woodlice, spiders, centipedes or even millipedes.

Look at what is growing on the bark, too. There are mosses, lichens and fungi growing all around the woodlands and they love damp, rotting bark and branches. Examine them more closely with the magnifying glass on the top of your finds tub and have a go at drawing them.

If you want to be scientific, you could make a small, square frame out of four twigs and record what insects, leaves, seeds, mosses, lichen and fungi you can find in that one square.

You can also use your binoculars to look up into the canopy for any birds that might be around. Blackbirds, wood pigeons, rooks and magpies are the bigger birds that you will see easily. Then look further down on the woodland floor. You might spot a little brown bird, that's probably a dunnock or a wren.

Make a note of what you find, so that once you are at home you can write your very own story about the life of the tree or shrubs you looked at.

What's the Time, Mr Wolf?

You will need at least three people to play this game. One of you pretends to be the wolf spider and the others are the ladybirds. The wolf spider stands in front of the other players with their back to them. The ladybirds stand a good distance away from the wolf spider.

The ladybirds start to slowly move forward and all ask together, 'What's the time, Mr Wolf?'

The wolf spider tells them the time, e.g.: 1, 2, 3, 4 o' clock. The ladybirds then move that number of steps forward. When the wolf spider decides to, they shout 'Dinner time!' instead of the time and the ladybirds run away.

The first ladybird to be tagged by the wolf spider is the next wolf spider and the game begins again. If a ladybird reaches the wolf spider before they have shouted, 'Dinner time!', they are the winner and can choose the next person to be wolf spider.

If you are outside, the person playing the wolf spider could hide behind a tree or a bush, just like the wolf spider who hides in the wall in the story, 'Who's Afraid of the Big Bad Wolf'.

The Magic of Nature

The world around us is full of magic, just as Sebastian discovered in 'Pulling it out of the Hat'. Here are a few magic tricks you can perform at home with a little help from nature.

Rainbow Flowers

Take some white flowers, for example, carnations, gerberas or roses. Cut the stems to around 10cm long and place them in cup with approximately 100ml of water. Carefully add a teaspoon of your chosen food colouring to the water. You could try several different colours in different cups to create a rainbow. Leave overnight, and in the morning your flowers will have changed colour. Colours that work well are green, blue, yellow and orange.

Cockleshells and pebbles

If you are near a beach, collect three large shells such as cockleshells or oyster shells. Find a small pebble that will fit under them all. Now find someone to play the game with you.

Find a flat surface to put the shells on. Place the stone under one of the shells and ask your friend to play close attention as you mix all three shells up. Now ask your friend which shell the pebble is under. Did they guess correctly?

A Juicy Message

You will need a small paintbrush or cotton wool bud, a slice of white bread, lemon juice and a toaster for this trick. Squeeze out some lemon juice into a pot. Take the slice of bread and write a message on it with the lemon juice, using the paintbrush or cotton wool bud. Let the lemon juice dry. Now, toast your bread and, hey presto, your secret message will appear.

Minestrone Soup

Serves 6

Originally from Italy, Minestrone soup can be made with a variety of different ingredients depending on what people have in their cupboards. Traditionally, it is a tomato-based vegetable soup with beans, pasta and/or rice. In this version we use orzo pasta, which is Italian for barley, as the tiny pasta shapes look like grains of barley.

Have fun with this recipe and experiment. Substitute spinach for kale, carrot for potato, basil for parsley or swap orzo pasta for rice. Use up what you have left in your cupboard, just like they do in the story of 'The Village Cauldron'.

Ingredients

1 small red onion
2 medium carrots
1 tbsp olive oil
1 clove garlic

½ tsp dried basil
1 vegetable stock cube
2 tsp tomato puree
2 tsp balsamic vinegar
1 × 400g can chopped tomatoes
1 × 400g can cannellini beans
600ml water
50g orzo pasta
100g baby spinach

Method

* Peel and finely slice the onion.
* Peel and dice the carrots.
* Add the olive oil to a large pan with the onion and carrots. Cook on a medium heat until they begin to soften. This should take about 10 minutes. Peel and crush the garlic.
* Add the garlic and cook for a further minute. Add the canned tomatoes, dried basil, tomato puree and balsamic vinegar to the pan and cook for a further 2–3 minutes.
* Add the stock cube to 600ml of boiling water and dissolve. Drain and rinse the cannellini beans. Add the cannellini beans and the stock to the pan. Bring to a simmer. Add the orzo pasta and simmer for 15 minutes or until the pasta is cooked through.
* Add the spinach, cook through, season with salt and pepper and serve with crusty bread and butter.

February

White bells of hope
Push through frosted ground
The woodland is awake
There are treasures to be found

Walk to the Beat of Your Own Drum

There once was a drummer boy who set out to find his fortune. He packed some bread and cheese in a handkerchief, slung his drum around his neck and off he went. He knew the path would be long, but he had time, and he would play his drum to keep pace along the way.

He hadn't gone far when a hawk heard the rat-ta-tat-tat of the drummer boy's drum and came down to see who it was.

'That is a fine rhythm you are playing there,' said the hawk, 'but if you play a little faster, I can beat my wings in time to the drum and catch us a rabbit for dinner.'

This was a great idea, thought the drummer boy, and he beat the sticks on the hide of the drum a little faster. With it, his pace quickened, and life felt good. After a day of walking, the hawk had caught them three rabbits and they stopped under an oak tree to cook and feast on their catch.

'Perhaps you will join me on my journey tomorrow?' the drummer boy asked.

'Gladly,' replied the hawk.

The next day, as the drummer boy and the hawk marched on, a dog, sleeping in a nearby barn, heard the drum's rhythm and stuck his head out of the barn door. He saw the companions and bounded up to them.

'Hello, friends,' he said, and then to the drummer boy, 'If you beat your drum a little faster, I can run with you and flush out the rabbits for the hawk.'

'A fabulous plan,' said the drummer boy, and he picked up the pace. Now he was running to keep up. The dog ran and the hawk swooped, and the rabbits dashed this way and that. By lunchtime they had caught five rabbits, but the drummer was exhausted, and his feet ached.

'I will have to rest,' he said. 'Let us camp here and enjoy the rabbits we have caught today.'

'Good idea,' said the dog and the hawk, and they all settled down to a grand meal.

The next day they started off again. The dog and the hawk kept up the pace and the drummer focused on the path ahead, lengthening his footsteps and striding on.

Soon they came upon a horse who was grazing in the meadow and he raised his head as he heard the drumbeat. He could see the drummer was tired and that the dog and the hawk were almost leaving him behind.

'If you quicken your drum,' said the horse, 'you can ride on my back and I will gallop in time. Then you will have no trouble keeping up with the hawk and the dog. I could do with an adventure and fresh new pastures!'

The drummer boy was not going to refuse. His feet were throbbing, and his shoes were almost threadbare. Mounting the horse, he began to play the drum faster still and they raced on through the country, the dog flushing out rabbits and the hawk catching one after another, after another.

These were good times, but the drummer boy had to concentrate hard to drum fast enough, and he was staring so intently at his drum that he did not see the low branch of a tree in front of them. They rode closer and closer until, bang! It knocked him off the horse.

As he lay there on his back, the hawk, the dog and the horse gathered around. 'What are you doing down there?' they asked.

The drummer boy got up and dusted himself off. Touching his head cautiously, he replied, 'I have a headache to match my sore feet, and look, my drumsticks are broken! You're all going too fast for me.'

'Oh no,' said the hawk, 'and we were doing so well. We have caught seven rabbits already.'

'I think,' replied the drummer boy, 'I had better go a little slower. Hawk, you are meant for hunting; dog, you are meant for running, and horse, you are meant for galloping, but I am meant for marching.'

The drummer boy rubbed the growing bump on his head and reached up into the tree for a suitable branch to make some new drumsticks.

'You have more than enough rabbits now,' he said, 'and I appreciate your help, but I will only hold you back. I will go on alone at my own pace.'

'Oh no!' squawked the hawk.

'Oh no!' barked the dog.

'Oh no!' neighed the horse.

'We are friends,' they all said, 'and we stick together. We will march to the beat of your drum, and for an hour a day, we can go a little faster to hunt for our supper.'

The drummer boy was very happy with this idea and hugged them all in turn. They continued along the path following the drummer's march. For one hour a day the hawk danced a reel above them, the dog ran with the wind in his ears to catch their food and the drummer boy rode upon the horse. They travelled for many days, hunting rabbits for their supper, until the drummer boy reached the town, where he did indeed make his fortune.

Still, to this day, they all live together in a little house on the outskirts of the town and every evening they dine on rabbit stew.

The Early Bee Collects the Pollen

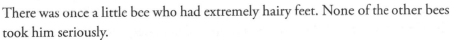

There was once a little bee who had extremely hairy feet. None of the other bees took him seriously.

'How do you not get stuck to the flowers with such hairy feet?' they would taunt.

'Are your wings beating twice as fast to lift the extra weight?' fuzzed the honeybees.

This teasing hurt the little bee's feelings and it made him worried about going to collect pollen in front of the other bees. He grew sad and lonely, and soon he just stayed in a hole near the bottom of the garden wall, where he'd made his home.

The blackbird that lived in the garden saw this and took to leaving fresh flowers by the little bee's front door to tempt him out. Eventually, one morning the bee got thirsty, and he crept from the wall and supped on the nectar in the flowers the blackbird had left.

'Hello, little bee,' called the blackbird. 'Why do you hide?'

The little bee was startled and looked up at the blackbird, the early morning sunlight making him squint.

'What are you doing up so early?' he demanded.

'The early bird catches the worm!' the blackbird replied.

'Very true.' The bee returned to his pollen and, once finished, went to crawl back to the hole in the wall.

'Wait a minute,' said the blackbird.

'Oh, I'm sorry. Thank you for the pollen,' the bee said, thinking the blackbird had thought him ungrateful.

'No, I just want to know why you hide?'

'The other bees laugh at my hairy feet.'

'Really? That's not nice. Surely, they are very good for collecting pollen, as it sticks to the little hairs?'

'Yes, they are!' The little bee smiled at the blackbird. Finally, someone understood.

'Then why miss out? The other birds used to laugh at me because I am all black with no bright colours, apart from the yellow on my beak. But I am the first to wake and the last to sleep. I am the keeper of this garden and in the half-light of dawn and dusk I am perfectly camouflaged. I get all the best worms!'

'I see. So, if I get up early and collect my pollen before all the other bees, I'll get the best pollen!'

'Exactly!' replied the blackbird.

The bee was happy in this thought and couldn't wait to get up the next day before all the other bees. This is why the hairy-footed flower bee is the first bee to emerge each year from hibernation. It works hard to collect the first of the new pollen while all the other bees are still fast asleep. So now the only bee laughing is the hairy-footed flower bee.

The Green Man of the Woods

There was once a celebrated traveller who rode a beautiful white horse whose coat shimmered in the dappled light of the woodland where they roamed. It was in a time when trees covered much of the land and often stretched as far as the eye could see.

The traveller spoke the language of woods. He could find you the right flower for any problem you may have had. He dressed in the subtle greens and browns of the woodland and if he did not want to be, he could not be seen, and so people called him Green Man. As far as they could tell, he was as old as the wood itself. People came from far and wide to ask for his advice, as only he truly understood each flower's message.

On this particular day, the first person to approach him was a young woman.

'How can I help you?' asked Green Man.

'My chickens are sitting on eggs and I wish to make sure they hatch safely. Is there a flower that can help me?' the young woman replied.

'There is a flower, but you must take care. The primrose will help if it sees fit, but if you take fewer than thirteen primrose flowers into your house, the hens will not hatch the eggs they brood. Take care,' Green Man said, as he pointed to a bank of bright yellow primroses the woman was sure had not been there before.

'Thank you,' replied the woman, and started to gather the primroses in her apron, counting them carefully as she did.

Riding further through the wood, Green Man met another traveller, this time a man who was stumbling and occasionally reaching out to lean on the stout tree trunks around him.

'Can I help you?' asked Green Man.

There was no mistaking the sound of Green Man's voice. It sang like the wind and held the words of many conversations.

'Green Man, is that you?' the man asked.

'It is.'

'Then I am lucky to have found you. My sight is failing, and yet I have many years ahead of me. I do not know what to do.'

'The juice of the celandine flower may help you. Squeeze the liquid from its petals and apply it to your eyes.'

'Thank you,' replied the man, as Green Man got down from his horse and helped him to gather the flowers he needed.

Next, Green Man came upon a young mother who was walking through the wood with her crying son.

'Why do you cry?' asked Green Man, of the son.

His mother replied. 'He swallowed one of his milk teeth and now I fear his new tooth will grow as long as a wolf's.'

'Do not worry. He must take a flower from the delicate dog violet and eat it. Then all will be well.'

The boy wiped the tears from his face and followed his mother to where there was a patch of dog violets, with their five purple petals and heart-shaped leaves.

'Thank you,' the mother smiled, grateful for Green Man's help.

That day, Green Man helped many more people in the woodland. He gave wood anemones to a man who wished to protect his cattle from disease, wild garlic to a woman for her aching hands tired from hard work and the leaves of a dock to a young girl who had been stung by nettles.

There were many ways Green Man helped the people he met on his travels. When they understood what nature could do for them, Green Man often found that people would look after the woodlands in return. That way, there would always be more plants to help them in the future. I haven't seen Green Man for many years, perhaps because there is less woodland for him to travel around these days.

Of course, now we have doctors we go to see if we are ill, but we still use our woodlands for other things: wood for fires and making paper and card, plants to feed the insects that pollinate our crops, and the trees give us vital oxygen as they breathe out so we can breathe in.

So, you see, it's just as important to look after the woodlands now as it was then, and who knows, if we do, perhaps Green Man will return.

The Little Goat Shepherd

On the other side of the world, there lived a little goat who was always being told what to do: 'Don't eat that … stand there … do as you're told.' He had a hard time of it, but he stayed with his herd because he was a loyal little goat.

One day, when the herd was grazing beside the mountains, a big sheep came bounding up. 'Have you heard about the wolf that's roaming these parts?'

'Noooo!' bleated the goats.

'He's eating every sheep and goat he can find, do beeee careful,' the sheep replied, and ran on into the mountains.

'That doesn't sound good at all,' said the biggest goat with huge curling horns. 'We need a lookout. Little goat! You're the smallest; you can go up that tree and keep a look out for us. The branches won't break under your weight.'

'But I'm hungry,' said the little goat.

'You can eat later, when we've all had our food and can watch for ourselves.'

'I'm afraid of heights,' said the little goat, who really was afraid of heights.

'No excuses,' bleated the big-horned goat.

There was no way the little goat was getting out of it, so he carefully put his front feet on the lowest branch of the tree, ready to climb.

'Come on,' bleated the big goat, and before the little goat had a chance to move any further, the big goat buffeted him up into the branches with his horns and the little goat landed on his face in among the leaves and berries. Picking himself up, he climbed the tree until he was at the top.

Looking around him, the mountains seemed at peace and there was no sign of the wolf. The little goat's lips felt wet, and he thought he must have split his lip when he landed on his face. Licking his mouth, he found not blood but a sweet-tasting juice. Glancing down at the tree branches, he saw tiny red berries and he realised this must be what he could taste. It wasn't long before he had eaten his fill and he looked up just in time to see the wolf coming out of the mountains.

'Wolf! wolf!' he called to the goats below and they ran in all directions, scattering in a panic. They could not run fast or climb the trees as their bellies were round and full of fresh grass. The little goat could do nothing except bleat as loudly as he could for the farmer to come and help.

That day, the wolf got many goats for his supper before the farmer finally arrived and chased him away, but the little goat was safe at the top of the tree and his tummy was full of juicy berries. He was grateful for his good fortune and, from that day on, he was content to be the lookout in the tree and feast on the fruits found there.

Activities

The Journey Stick

For centuries, people have been taking journeys and voyages of discovery; sometimes to find new lands and sometimes to learn something new about themselves. Stories are journeys of discovery, just like the one in 'Walk to the Beat of Your Own Drum'. Everyone sees different things, hears different sounds, smells different smells and feels different textures as they walk through the world.

A journey stick is something that is used by the Aboriginals, the indigenous people of Australia, and it is a way of recording what you find on your journey. All you will need to begin your adventure is some pieces of wool or string, ready cut.

Decide where you want to go. Do you want to travel through the ancient woodlands, climb a mountain that's as old as the sky or rediscover your garden or park?

Next, you need to find yourself a sturdy stick about 20–30cm long.

As you take your walk, look around at the plants and animals, the nooks and crannies in the walls or rocks, the gravel, mud or leaves beneath your feet. How do they make you feel? What can you hear? What can you smell? Do the different colours and textures remind you of anything?

Every now and then, you may see something that you would like to collect to record your journey: a seed head, a feather, a leaf, a flower, a pebble. If it is OK to do so (always ask an adult first and follow the Countryside Code – there is a link to the code in the back of this book), then you can take the item and use a piece of the wool or string to attach it to your stick. This will become your journey stick. Continue to collect things until your stick is full or your adventure has come to an end. Once you have returned home, tell a story with the items you have found, and tell people about your adventures, because now, wrapped around this wonderful little stick is your story.

If you don't have a green space that you can access easily, you could try doing this around the house. Use a ruler or a wooden spoon and attach items using wool and string. Again, you can tell a story with them. If you don't want to attach items to the string, or the items are too big, try using parcel tags and write on them what you have found or draw a picture of it.

Enjoy your journey!

Early Bee Watch

In February the animals and insects that have been dormant or hibernating all winter start to wake up. Just like in 'The Early Bee Catches the Pollen', the hairy-footed flower bee is one of the first to appear. The bees appearing now are solitary bees without a colony, who live alone all year round, or great big queen bumblebees, who are the only bees from their colony to survive over the winter.

For this activity, you will need to find a spot in the garden or your local green space and sit and watch for the bees. Take your Adventure Journal with you, so you can make a note of what you see. If you can't get to a green space, try putting a few potted plants by the front door or in a window box. Spring bulbs like crocuses are good for attracting bees or, if you have a little more space, a shrub such a hebe or skimmia are bee heaven.

Here are some of the bees you might spot:

Early Bumblebee

Early bumblebees have a classic yellow collar, black middle (sometimes with a yellow band), and a dark yellow/orange tail. Their hair is long, so they appear very fluffy and slightly dishevelled. They are around 1cm in size.

Hairy-Footed Flower Bee

The female hairy-footed flower bee is completely black apart from her legs, which have orange pollen brushes on them, hence the name hairy-footed bee. She is medium in size at between 1 and 2cm. The males are a brown colour, have a white face and hairs on their middle pair of feet.

Ashy Mining Bee

The ashy mining bee tends to nest in the ground and, like the hairy-footed flower bee, is another small solitary bee. It is just over 1cm. You might be lucky enough to spot these on an early dandelion. If you see a little black bee with grey bands, it's likely to be an ashy mining bee.

White-Tailed Bumblebee

The queen white-tailed bumblebee is twice the size of a worker bee and is one of the bigger bumblebees you can spot out and about in the flowerbeds in early spring. Their white fluffy tails and black and yellow stripes make them easy to spot.

Red-Tailed Bumblebee

The red-tailed bumblebee has a black body and black pollen baskets on its feet. Again, it is about the same size as its white-tailed cousin but has a dark orange tail, giving it the name 'red-tailed'.

If you do spot bees on your Early Bee Watch, then be sure to record which ones you see and you could even help the Bumblebee Conservation Trust by submitting your recorded finds using this web address: www.bumblebeeconservation.org/surveys. They also have some excellent bee guides you can download to help you with your Early Bee Watch.

Pause as the Wheel Turns

Imbolc

There are eight sabbats in the ancient Celtic wheel of the year: four solar festivals and four farming festivals. The Imbolc (pronounced ee-molc) is the first of the farming festivals. It celebrates the life that is about to arrive with the spring as the days grow noticeably longer and the smell of fresh grass hangs in the air. The word Imbolc is thought to derive from the old Irish for 'in the belly', referring to the lambs that the ewes now carry. It is also related to old European words that mean 'ewe's milk'. The next two activities celebrate the life we find in the fields at this time of year.

In the circle of life, the shepherd and farmer spend long hours protecting their flock, respecting and caring for the life in the fields. This life, in turn, can give us sustenance in the form of food and milk, sheepskins to keep us warm and soap to cleanse our skin.

Goat's Milk Soap with Peppermint and Primrose

This recipe uses a melt-and-pour goat's milk soap. You can use any soap base and add dried goat's milk to the soap, but you will need to mix the dried milk with water to make a thin paste first and add it gradually to the soap base to prevent clumping.

There are many places that sell soap bases and soap-making ingredients online and in some larger high street craft shops, so you don't need to worry about using chemicals like lye.

Goat's milk is great for dry skin battered by the winter weather and this recipe uses peppermint to raise the spirits as we wait for spring to arrive. When you're out on a walk, as Green Man does, look out for the flowers that are appearing in the woodlands, parks and gardens. The primroses will be starting to appear, and you could pick a primrose flower or two to place in the soap. Primroses are edible but, as with anything new, it is important to make sure you are not going to have a reaction to it first, so rub a petal on the inside of your wrist and leave it for twenty-four hours to check. It is also important to know what you are picking and only pick what you need.

Ingredients
700g melt-and-pour goat's milk soap
10 drops peppermint essential oil
primrose flowers (optional)
6 × 125g cavity silicone soap moulds

Method
* In a large pan that you aren't using for cooking, melt the soap gently on a very low heat. Once it is completely melted, add the peppermint oil to the melted soap base and stir gently.
* Pour the liquid into the soap mould and add a primrose flower to the top of each one.
* Push the flower gently into the soap with the end of a teaspoon or a cocktail stick.
* Allow the soaps to cool and harden before wrapping in parchment and storing in a cool dry place.

Shepherd's Pie

Serves 4

This is a recipe to warm the bones of those who spend their days in the fields and hills, looking after the livestock. There are many versions of shepherd's pie but it always contains lamb. In this version, the mashed potato is on the bottom, sides and the top of the pie, as can be found in 1907 version of Mrs Beeton's famous cookbook. You can make this pie vegetarian by using a vegetarian mince substitute. You could also use left-over roast lamb or even goat, just don't let the little goat shepherd know or he'll never come out of that tree.

Ingredients

1kg white potatoes
3 tbsp olive oil
salt and pepper
½ tsp dried parsley
1 small red onion, diced
2 carrots, diced or grated
400g lamb mince
1 clove garlic, crushed (or more, if you like garlic, you could even see if you can find some wild garlic although it may be a little early)
1 tbsp tomato puree
1 tsp chives
1 tbsp Worcester sauce
400g can chopped tomatoes
200ml water
handful of grated cheese to top (optional)

Method

* Preheat the oven to 180°C.
* Peel and cube the potatoes. Place in a large pan with water and a pinch of salt. Bring to the boil and cook until soft. Drain the potatoes and roughly mash with 2 tbsp of the olive oil. Add the parsley, salt and pepper to taste. Put to one side until ready to use.

✱ Finely dice the onion and peel and dice the carrots.

✱ Heat the remaining oil in a large frying pan. Fry the lamb on a high heat until it is brown. Place the lamb in a dish to one side, retaining the juices in the frying pan.

✱ Turn the heat down and fry the onion and carrots for around 10 minutes until both are softening. Add extra oil if required.

✱ Add the crushed garlic (or finely chopped wild garlic) and fry for about a minute. Now add the lamb, tinned tomatoes, water, tomato puree, Worcester sauce and chives. Bring the mixture to the boil and then turn down to a simmer, stirring occasionally to prevent it sticking. Simmer for 20 minutes until the ingredients are well combined and cooked through. Add extra water if required.

✱ While the lamb mixture is cooking, prepare a medium-sized baking dish. Take half of the potato mixture and line the dish with it, pushing it up the sides as well.

✱ Once the lamb mixture is cooked through, add it to the baking dish and layer the remaining potato on the top. You can grate a little cheese over the top, if you would like, or use a fork to create lines in the potato that will crisp up in the oven.

✱ Bake in the oven for 20–30 minutes, until golden on top. You might want to place it on a baking tray to catch any bubbling loveliness trying to escape the pie. Serve with fresh spring peas or salad.

March

Burgeoning bird song
Fills cloud soft skies
Join the throng
As nature thrives

Little Fish with the Golden Tail

Once upon a time, there was a little fish with the most magnificent tail; a long, forked swirl of gold, glinting in the cool blue pond that was his home. Every day the fish would swim through the reeds and catch a glimpse of his tail. Then, in a flurry of bubbles and froth, he'd dash around the pond.

'What are you doing?' asked Frog.

'Can you see the gold?' said Little Fish. 'I'm trying to pick it up so I can hide it away from anyone who might try to steal it. Every day I try and every day I fail.'

Frog looked hard at Little Fish, who was earnest in his quest. 'That's your tail, Little Fish,' said Frog, frowning.

'No it's not. Surely you can see it's a treasure chest of gold?'

Before Frog could say any more, Little Fish asked, 'Perhaps you can leap onto it from your lily pad?'

'But you already have the gold,' replied Frog.

But Little Fish insisted and so Frog jumped off his lily pad and tried to catch the fish's tail. As he jumped, Little Fish moved to get out of his way. Whoosh! Frog missed. Frog could not catch Little Fish's golden fins.

A thousand tiny bubbles floated to the surface and caught the attention of Water Boatman, skimming along the water.

'What's going on down there?' he shouted.

'I'm trying to get hold of this gold,' Little Fish replied. 'Frog is too slow. Can you help?'

'That's your tail,' giggled Water Boatman.

'No it's not,' said Little Fish, who was really quite grumpy now. 'You're faster than Frog. Can you catch it?'

Well, Water Boatman was fond of a game and so he chased Little Fish's tail, knowing full well he was never going to catch it.

'It's no use,' flounced Little Fish. 'Frog is too slow. Water Boatman's too slow. I need someone faster. I know, I'll go and ask Pike.'

Frog and Water Boatman put their heads in their hands. Pike was the biggest, ugliest, meanest fish in the pond – not a fish to be trifled with – but Little Fish with the golden tail wouldn't be told.

Swimming into the murky depths at the centre of the pond, through the woven lily stems and knotted duckweed, Little Fish found Pike. He gave a little cough. 'Ahem. Pike, sorry to disturb you, but can you help me catch this gold?'

Pike stretched his fins and peered at Little Fish. 'That's your tail!' his voice boomed, sending ripples around the lake, and a large bubble floated up to the surface and popped.

'No it's not, it's a treasure chest. Please help me catch it. I'll give you a gold coin for your trouble.'

'Ha ha!' laughed Pike, for never had a meal come right up to him and asked to be eaten. 'Alright', he said, and rushed at Little Fish, who dashed ahead trying to get out of Pike's way so Pike could catch the gold.

Round the duckweed, through the lily stems and into the bulrushes; finally, Pike caught hold of Little Fish's tail. Chomp!

'Yaoooooooo!' cried Little Fish and pulled with all his might. Only just managing to get himself free, he shot up high over the pond, past Frog on his lily pad, past the skating Water Boatman, high, high into the sky and into a neighbouring pond.

Little Fish was safe, but there was now a piece the size of a small coin missing from his beautiful tail. Little Fish now realised that Frog, Water Boatman and Pike were all telling the truth. The treasure was his tail and Pike had taken his nugget of gold.

Next time you peer into a pond, see if you can see a little fish with a tiny bit missing from his golden tail and heed the warning: sometimes it's a good idea to believe those who can see things that perhaps you can't.

A Love of the Light

There was once a little moth who loved another moth with all his heart, but she did not return his feelings. She loved the light.

She danced all night around the solar-powered lights that lined the gravel pathway of the garden where the little moths lived. She ignored the little moth's gifts of tiny blossoms, nectar and fairy dust. She was blind to anything but the light.

Summer is fleeting, and soon the solar lights began to fade. The little moth moved her attentions to the streetlamps standing tall beside the pavement outside the houses. She danced once more and ignored the other moth when he brought her gifts of gossamer shawls and dewdrop necklaces. But soon, the bulb on the streetlamp ran out of energy and the moth had to look elsewhere.

Over the rooftops at the back of town a football stadium was alive with life but it wasn't the cheering crowds that drew the little moth. It was the large stadium lights glowing in the darkness. She flew towards them and her suitor followed, bringing leaves, this time, to build a place for them to hibernate for winter was here. But she did not look back.

The match played on, the moth danced and soon the people went home. One by one, the lights were turned off.

Far away on the horizon the little moth saw a light brighter than any other she had known. She flew on and on and eventually arrived at the edge of some rocks. Towering above her were the strobing beams of a lighthouse. This was truly the most magnificent light and she danced as she had never danced before.

Around and around the light she went and, as she did, the wind started to pick up and the sea crashed against the rocks. A terrible storm had arrived, and the wind swirled and whirled, picking the little moth up and flinging her this way and that until she came to rest on top of the cliff.

The sky was black and ominous, and as the little moth came to, out of the rain and hail came her suitor moth. Picking her up out of the damp grass, he flew with her in his arms to his little moth house and cooked her warming clover blossom soup with the last of the summer flowers. When they had finished, he took her to the door of his house and pointed up to the sky.

There in the sky was the most beautiful light to behold. The moon was full and bright and shone right into the little moth's house. It was at this moment that she realised she had been chasing a light for so long, she had forgotten to open her eyes and see what was before her – a little moth who loved her and had given her the moon.

The Perfect Place to Sleep

Once upon a time, there was a tooth fairy who had been up all night collecting teeth from under children's pillows, casting dream spells for them and showering fairy dust on the stars above them. The teeth were to be made into fairy castles and pathways and she was carrying them home, but she was very tired and very much needed a place to rest before going any further.

The first flower she came to was a daisy. Its white petals were curled over a soft bed of yellow pollen. It looked like the perfect place to sleep, so she crawled under the petals and quickly drifted off. But it was not to be. The heat of the sun soon woke her as the petals of the daisy unfolded and the day began.

'Oh no,' grumped the fairy, and slid off the flower. 'I will have to find somewhere else to sleep.'

Next, she found the soft, sweet-smelling flowers of the lavender. She could tuck herself into the flowers away from the sun and snuggle down. So she did. But by mid-morning, she was rudely awoken by the loud buzzing of the bees.

'Buzz off!' shouted the fairy.

'But these are our favourite flowers,' replied the bees. 'And without their pollen we cannot make honey for your cakes.'

Now, the fairy's favourite thing was lavender honey cake and so she sighed, knowing she would have to find another flower to sleep in. 'Very well,' she said, as she got out of the lavender and went to find a more peaceful place.

After a bit more walking, she found a bluebell flower whose petals formed the perfect-sized fairy bed. 'Just right,' thought the fairy, and she climbed in. But she found she wasn't sleepy anymore.

She was about to give up and fly home when a gentle breeze rocked the bluebell flower to and fro and the bells tinkled. She found the soft sound and the gentle rocking soothing and, in no time, she was asleep.

So, next time you pass a bluebell, make sure you're very quiet so as not to wake the fairy sleeping inside.

The Wren's Choice

In a wood not too far from here lives a wren. He is a small and mighty bird. His shrill trill can be heard for many miles and he is considered the king of the holly hedge where he lives. On the other side of the wood, not too far away, is a row of farmer's cottages and a big house, which is the farmer's. Surrounding the houses are the fields that the farmer ploughs and tends.

Spring has come, and while the farmer is busy out in the fields, the wren is busy too.

You see, wrens must prepare several nests to attract female wrens. Once he has built his nests in places he thinks are suitable, the female wren chooses one of the nests. This is the story of how the little wren found the perfect nest.

This year, the wren was building three nests and he busied himself, flitting this way and that, gathering suitable nesting material. First, he built a little round nest at the bottom of the hedge with straw and long grass from the farmer's field. Next, he went to the holly bush that was his home and used moss and leaves to make repairs to last year's nest. Finally, he went to the farmer's house where he knew there was a hole in the wall near the wooden window frame that looked out on to the pond. The little fountain in the pond glistened in the sunshine and he thought it looked very pretty. He placed moss and feathers and lichen in this nesting place and, pleased with his work, he stepped back to admire it.

'Well, if my Jenny Wren wants a field view, she can have one from the hedge. If she wants a woodland view, she has one from the holly bush. Or if those won't please her, surely the view of this magnificent garden will,' he said to himself, looking out across the manicured lawn and the perfectly pruned rose bushes.

The wren went back to the first nest, called to the Jenny Wren and waited. Sure enough, soon she arrived to inspect the nests.

He showed her to the nest in the hedge first. Jenny Wren hopped from branch to branch looking this way and that across the field and into the long grass that grew around the hedge.

'I must admit,' she said, 'this is a fine spot with a beautiful view, and you have made a good job of weaving this nest but look, look closely at the long grass.'

As the wren did, he saw what Jenny Wren was looking at. Curled up under the hedge was an adder basking in the evening sun. The snake of the hedgerow would surely eat their eggs should it get the chance.

'Quite right, my Jenny,' the wren replied. 'Let me show you the next nest.'

They flew on to the holly bush in the wood and Jenny Wren hopped this way and that, inspecting the nest and the surroundings. 'This too has a fine view, and it is homely,' Jenny Wren agreed, 'but listen, can you hear?'

And it was then the wren did hear.

'Cuckoo! Cuckoo!'

'Oh no,' the wren replied. 'You are right, dear Jenny, the cuckoo will surely lay eggs in our nest and we will run ourselves ragged feeding her young. Never fear, this last nest is sure to satisfy our requirements.'

They flew on to the nest in the wall of the farmer's grand house. The rose garden was starting to bud, and the ivy-covered wall offered excellent protection and cover. With a pond in front of it, there would be plenty of insects visiting the water that they could eat. Jenny Wren hopped this way and that, and she was just about to settle when the fountain sprang into life, the water shooting high into the air and then showering down on the pond, splashing the wall of the house and leaving tiny droplets of water on the moss and lichen that made up the little nest wren had made.

'This will not do,' Jenny said. 'The eggs will get wet and cold, we cannot nest here.'

'What are we to do?' the wren asked, 'I have nowhere else to show you.'

'I know of somewhere,' said Jenny Wren. 'If you will follow me.'

And so, the little wren did, and they flew over the farmer's house, down the lane and into the garden of one of the farm cottages. There, on a sunny wall was a nesting box, just the right size for a wren. Beside it was a compost heap full of things they could use for their nest and full of insects they could eat and feed to their young.

The wren got to work immediately building a nest inside the box, and when he was done, Jenny Wren lined the nest with soft feathers.

Soon they had seven little speckled eggs, which all hatched that spring. The two wrens worked together to feed their brood with insect after insect from the compost heap, and if they haven't finished feeding them now, then I should think they are still feeding them.

Activities

Pond Dipping

Spring is here and all the animals are waking up, creatures of the earth, air and water. This activity explores the local wildlife found in water, in particular ponds. Pond dipping is a great way to find out what's living in the water near you, but you could also try a stream or slow-flowing river.

Always remember to stay safe near water and take an adult with you to help.

What you will need:
* appropriate clothing and footwear (it can get very muddy and slippery underfoot near water)
* a net or jar
* a small bucket or seed tray without holes in it

✸ a good pond or wildlife guide (the RSPB has a great pond-dipping guide, which you can find a link to in the back of the book)
✸ your Adventure Journal and pen to note your finds.

How to pond dip:

Find a suitable spot where you can reach the water safely. Spend some time quietly observing the water and the creatures coming and going in the pond. This way, you can see what there is to try and catch.

Now, use your net or jar to gently scoop some water out of the pond. If you are using a net, tip the contents into a small bucket filled with the same pond water. If you are using a jar, you can observe the creatures through the glass.

You may find many little creatures in the water, and once you've had a look and identified them, it's important to carefully pour them back into the pond.

It is also important to bear in mind that some animals, for example newts, are protected species as there are not many of them left, so it's best to observe them from your pond-side vantage point rather than scooping them out of the water.

Always make sure that if your hands have been in the water, you do not put them near your face until you have cleaned them. When you get home, soak your net or jar in hot water and give it a good clean to make sure it's ready for your next adventure.

As an extra activity, you could put together a bingo-style sheet with nine animals you might find down at your pond or river. While you're there, tick off the animals you find and see who can find them all first. And don't forget, if you peer into the water and spot a fish with a golden tail that has a small chunk missing from it, you know who it is!

What animals and pond life to spot in March:

✸ mallards
✸ frogs
✸ toads
✸ early darters
✸ newts
✸ frog and toad spawn
✸ whirligig beetles
✸ pond skaters
✸ midge larvae
✸ water spiders
✸ fish – stickleback, perch or carp

Moth Hunt

There are around 2,500 species of moth in the UK, and at this time of year many moths are coming out of their winter hibernation. The evenings are getting lighter, but it is still dark enough to squeeze in a moth hunt before it gets too late. As we saw in the story of the moth who could not resist the light, moths are drawn to the light. The scientific name for this is phototaxis and we can use this reaction to observe moths a little closer.

For this super simple activity, you will need the following:

* washing line, wall or fence
* old white sheet
* torch
* wildlife guide that includes moths (there is a link to an online moth guide in the back of this book).

Choose a still evening that is a little warmer than usual for your moth hunt. Try to find a place where there are no other artificial lights. If it's your back garden, turn off any outside lights and the indoor ones that are peeking through the curtains. Hang your old white sheet on the washing line or attach it to the wall or fence. Now, stand a few feet back from the sheet and shine the torch onto it. Watch the moths come to the light and see how many you can identify.

Pause as the Wheel Turns

Ostara

Spring is most definitely here. The trees explode with bird song, all around the creatures gather nesting materials and the cloud-soft sky gives way to bright sunshine. This is the time of new life; the time when balance is restored – the time of the equinox.

Ostara, also known as Eostre, is celebrated between 19 and 21 March, when the day and the night are equal, and from now until late June, the sun will shine just a little brighter and a little longer each day. This festival is often seen as a celebration of the first day of spring and, indeed, many firsts – the first lambs are in the fields, the bulbs planted last year are first to be blazing in the borders and the first migrating birds are returning for the summer.

The Saxons celebrated this festival in honour of their goddess, Eostre, the bringer of new life, and her name can be translated as sun. The hare and the egg were symbols used in this festival and the Saxons would often hide eggs and then hunt them out. These were the first ever Easter egg hunts, almost fourteen hundred years ago.

Now is the time to sow seeds so that we may reap the rewards in the summer and the next activity is all about just that.

Magical Marigolds

There are many spring flowers blooming in the fields and woodlands at this time of year, but why not make a little space for flowers at home, too. Marigolds bloom orange and yellow like the sun and hold much folklore and magic, which they will, in turn, bring to your garden.

You can plant marigolds straight into the ground outside at this time of year, but if you don't have a garden you could plant up a pot for the windowsill, outside beside the front door or even in a window box.

Marigolds are magical flowers with tiny curling seeds that are easy to grow. Their yellow and orange petals bring the sunshine, even when the clouds hide the real sun away, and because they are in the daisy family, their petals open and close with the sun just like the daisy petals in 'The Perfect Place to Sleep'.

In some parts of the UK, it is thought that if a marigold does not open its petals before seven in the morning, there will be a thunderstorm that day. Once you've grown your marigold, you can test that theory and, who knows, perhaps a fairy will come and have a snooze in it ...

You will need:
* small pot with drainage holes in the bottom
* saucer or tray to put your pot on
* potting compost
* marigold seeds, which are available in most garden centres (or they are easy to collect from last year's marigolds if you know someone who has some)

Planting your marigolds:

Take the pot and fill it almost to the top with compost. Place four or five seeds in the pot and cover with a bit more compost. Gently pat down the compost and place the pot on the saucer/tray. Dampen the soil with a little water, but not too much. Don't be tempted to make puddles, no matter how much fun they are. Keep the soil wet to the touch, but not soaked, by watering a little every day until the marigold starts to grow.

As the marigold grows, you can use a small bamboo skewer and some string to stake it. To do this, push the skewer into the soil and use the string to tie the marigold loosely to the skewer.

If the marigold gets too big for the pot, you can always transfer it to a bigger pot. To do this, find a slighter bigger pot and add a little potting compost to the bottom of it. Gently remove the marigold from the first pot with the soil still on its roots and place it on top of the soil in the second, filling in any gaps with more potting compost. Gently push the compost down and water.

Alternatively, you can just plant your Marigold seeds straight outside in the ground. Find a suitable spot in the garden and create a little channel in the soil that runs the length of the area where you want the marigolds to grow. Scatter the seeds evenly in the channel and cover over with soil. Water the soil and then water every day after until the marigolds begin to appear.

By the summer months you should have a magnificent, magical and merry marigold plant on your windowsill or in your garden.

Noodle Nests

Makes 12

In the story of the little wren, the wren must make several nests to find the perfect one for his mate. Below, you can have a go at creating your own perfect little nest and this one's edible!

Ingredients

200g dry noodles
250g chestnut mushrooms
2 tbsp sunflower oil
3 spring onions

1 sweet red pepper
¼ tsp ground ginger
1 clove garlic
ground smoked paprika to garnish

Method

* ✳ Preheat your oven to 180°C. Cook the noodles as directed on the packet.
* ✳ Once cooked, drain using a sieve or colander and divide the noodles between the twelve sections of a muffin tin. Curl the noodles around in each mould to create the nest shape. Place the noodle nests in the oven for 15 minutes, until gold brown. Remove from the oven and leave to cool.
* ✳ While the noodles are cooking, thinly slice the mushrooms, finely dice the pepper and slice the spring onions.
* ✳ Heat two tablespoons of sunflower oil in a large frying pan and add the vegetables to the pan. Fry for 5 minutes while you peel and crush the garlic and then add this to the pan. Add the ground ginger and cook for a further 3 minutes. Remove from the heat.
* ✳ Place your noodle nests on a serving dish and spoon the vegetables into the middle of the noodles. Sprinkle with a little smoked paprika to taste and serve.

April

This is April full of change
The rain still falls and storms do rage
Yet birds build nests for coming young
And Hawthorn blooms for warmer days

A Land Without Snow

In a very hot country, far, far away, lives a little girl who longs for snow. She has never thrown a snowball, never built a snowman and never laid down in the snow and felt it cold against her body as she moves her arms and legs to make a snow angel. Her name is Constance.

One stifling summer, Constance longed for the cold and decided to go looking for the snow. First, she asked the old woman drawing water from the well, 'Where can I find snow?'

'In far off lands, many miles from here,' the old woman replied. She looked at Constance's face, red with the heat, and frowned, 'Here, have some water. Sit, and be content with what you have, my child.'

But Constance was far from content. She took a sip of the water, thanked the lady and went on her way. Soon, she saw a farmer tending to his crops of sweetcorn.

'Where can I find snow?' she asked.

'In far off lands, many miles from here,' the farmer replied. Red in the face from her travels in the heat of the day, Constance looked out of breath and the farmer encouraged her to rest. 'Here, have some corn. Sit, be content with what you have, my child.'

But Constance was far from content. She took some of the corn, thanked the farmer and went on her way.

She walked on through the countryside until she saw a cat basking in the sun on an old stone wall. She stopped to stroke it and, not really expecting any kind of an answer, she sighed and said, 'Where can I find snow, Cat?'

'Just over the hill,' purred the cat. 'Where the wind blows and the blossom grows.'

Constance's eyes were as round as saucers as she looked upon the talking cat. It stood up and stretched. 'Come with me and I will show you.'

Constance's heart was full of hope as she ran with the cat across the field and over the hill. Her ribbon fell out of her hair and flew away as the wind hustled around them.

'Here,' said the cat, arriving at a cherry tree.

'But this is just an old cherry tree,' replied Constance. She had seen many of these and while their fruit was good, they were not snow. 'There is no snow here.'

The cat jumped up into the tree. 'Wait for the wind to blow,' he replied.

Constance didn't have to wait long. A fresh breeze rippled through the cherry tree, shaking loose the petals of the tiny pink flowers and showering them onto the ground. Constance looked up, laughing and dancing, catching great handfuls of the cherry blossom and throwing them up in the air, again and again. She piled it against the old tree trunk and then spread it out again to lie down in it and make an angel shape. The petals were cool against her face and the smell of cherry blossom enveloped her. Finally, she had found snow.

Stormy Weather

There once was a time when the wind and the rain were great friends. When the wind twirled, the raindrops danced, and when the clouds released their showers, the wind scattered them over the crops, settling them on the parched ground where they would do the most good.

The animals and people of the Earth never feared the wind or the rain. They knew the rain came when it was needed and in the correct quantity. And they knew that the wind only blew the lightest of breezes to float the rain to where it should be.

This continued for many years until, one day, a tiny raindrop spoke out. 'Wind, why do you push us around? I want to travel the world, to take in the sights, but with you blowing us this way and that, we have no choice in the matter.'

'But I only rock you with the softest of breaths,' countered the wind.

'But never where we want,' replied the stubborn raindrop.

'It is where you are needed. Where the people and the animals of the Earth need you most.'

'Who are you to decide that? Surely the people and the animals should?'

'OK,' said the wind, 'we'll let them decide. Let us ask them.'

And so the wind and the rain shouted down to the animals and the people of the Earth, 'Where shall we go?'

'This way,' said the people.

'No, that way,' said the animals.

'But we have no water for our crops,' said the people.

'And we are thirsty,' said the animals.

Well, the wind blew backwards and forwards, getting dizzier and dizzier, spinning and swirling and curling above the world, whipping the raindrops with it.

'We are still being told what to do!' shouted the little raindrop.

The other raindrops agreed, and they puffed themselves out to become huge grey drops pushing against the wind, falling wherever they wanted, rivulets running down mountains, gathering pace and flooding valleys.

'Stop!' thundered the wind, as he lost control and spun upwards and upwards in a towering grey funnel, the rain spilling out around him.

'We will not!' screeched the rain, dancing faster and faster around the wind.

'Stop!' shouted the people, scared their crops would be washed away.

'Stop!' shouted the animals, terrified that their homes and burrows would be filled with water.

After a time, the rain did cease. But not until the drops had danced themselves out of their frenzy and gathered back into grey ominous clouds that laughed at the wind. The wind unwound out of his knot, and went to rest in the mountains, furious with the rain.

From that day forth, the wind and the rain have never been friends. The rain never dances in the wind and the wind will never more be gentle with the rain. Each storm is a reminder that we should not take the weather for granted. Occasionally the wind blows a terrible gale to remind the rain of its strength, and in return, the rain gathers in mass and volume, drenching the countryside, wherever it pleases as a reminder to the wind that it is free.

Dämmerung the Grey

Once upon a different time, there lived fairies for every colour of the rainbow. Red fairies danced on the roses and poppies in the field, yellow fairies painted sunshine through the leaves of the trees, orange fairies tiptoed across the citrus fruits in orchards and the green fairies ran through the lush meadows and fields. In the sky, blue fairies sang to the rain, and the lilac fairies spent their days snoozing in the bluebells and campanulas of the hedgerow.

But this story is about a little fairy who wasn't any of those colours. He was grey.

Dämmerung was born on a solar eclipse, a very rare occurrence when the Sun is hidden behind the Moon. The Earth had fallen silent and dark, just as

Dämmerung was born. Even as a tiny fairy, he was aware that he was different. While others danced and sang, he stayed in the shadows and the twilight where he felt safe, and the Sun would not burn his delicate wings. The only time he ventured out in the day was when it rained. Then, he would jump and twirl and shout to the skies of his happiness, dancing in the giant raindrops sent from his blue brothers.

They, too, were pleased to see him and let it rain for as long as they could, but the sunshine needed its turn too and so it was that Dämmerung's time would always come to an end. He would return to the shadows and await the next storm.

The other fairies desperately wanted to help Dämmerung but they couldn't see a way, until one day the Sun spoke up. 'Why do I never see Dämmerung?' she asked. 'He deserves light in his life and yet he hides in the shadows.'

'Your rays burn his delicate wings,' the fairies replied. 'He is not like us. We want to help him but Dämmerung cannot dance in the sun as we do. He only comes out in the rain.'

'I have an idea,' said the Sun and she whispered it to the blue fairies, who nodded their heads eagerly.

The next day the Sun was shining fiercely on the Earth, but the blue fairies were high up in the sky making raindrops and were getting ready to shake the clouds. As they finished, they looked to the Sun.

'Now?' they asked.

'Now!' replied the Sun.

Together, the Sun shone with all her might and the blue fairies jumped on the clouds. As the first drops of rain hit the ground, Dämmerung peered out of the shadows. It was sunny, but the rain was here again! He would have to jump from drop to drop to stop the Sun burning his wings, but he longed to feel the rain again and so he took a tiny step out and began to dance.

The Sun looked down and smiled to see Dämmerung's ballet. She concentrated her rays through the raindrops and created a rainbow that surrounded the grey fairy. It turned him red, orange, yellow, green, blue, indigo, violet and so much more. Dämmerung was so busy hopping between the puddles that he didn't notice.

As the rain stopped, Dämmerung prepared to go back to the edge of the woodland where it was dark and damp and the shadows would protect him, but as he walked he caught his reflection in the rivulets of water running along the field tracks. He couldn't believe his eyes. He was no longer the grey Dämmerung born on the eclipse; he was a multicoloured fairy with dazzling, iridescent wings. Tilting his head, he shouted to the Sun and the rain.

'Thank you!' he said, 'Thank you! Thank you! Now I no longer have to hide, I can work beside my brothers and sisters to bring colour and joy to the world.'

The Sun smiled. Her job was done. And so it was that Dämmerung was the first in a line of rainbow fairies who light up the world wherever there is a need for it, and never again will a fairy hide in the shadows.

The Weather Pig

On an island across the sea, there is a farm that sits on the hill and on that farm, there is a pig farmer named Carter. He owns many pigs. Saddlebacks, Gloucester Old Spots, Pot-Bellied, Large Blacks, Middle Whites – you name it, he has it. He loves pigs.

His favourite was an Oxford Sandy and Black, a lovely orangey-brown pig with big black spots. His name was Plum Pudding. He was one of the oldest pigs on the island, thought to be one hundred years old, but of course no one really believed that. Only Farmer Carter knew how old Plum Pudding was and he wasn't telling anyone.

So why was Plum Pudding called Plum Pudding, I hear you ask. Well, here's the tale.

Plum Pudding was a weather pig. A very special kind of pig that could tell you if it was going to rain or shine. Plum Pudding was particularly good at predicting storms. This was incredibly helpful to the villagers as it meant they could board up their windows, stoke the fires and make sure the field gates were closed so their livestock and produce were protected from the coming weather. The storms didn't come very often – maybe once or twice a year – but when they did, they could cause a lot of damage, and with Plum Pudding around it meant they always had minimal damage to the village.

How did Plum Pudding do this? If it was going to rain, Farmer Carter noted that Plum Pudding's tail was particularly curly. If it was going to be sunny, Plum Pudding would insist on going out into the field to romp around in the buttercups and daisies. However, if a storm was coming, Plum Pudding would not come out of his sty. He would stay in the little stone shelter and pile up the hay as high as it would go. The higher the pile of hay, the worse the storm was going to be.

On this occasion, Farmer Carter's pig, who had no name at that point, had spent every day for a week piling up the straw in his sty. Every day, the villagers would board up the windows, close the gates and stoke the fires, but the storm never came. So, they'd take the boards off the windows, open up the gates and damp down the fires, until the next day when Plum Pudding would add more hay to his sty and they'd have to do it all again. Farmer Carter thought the pig had lost his talent.

'Perhaps it's going to be the worst storm in history,' Mrs Farmer Carter warned.

'I'm not so sure,' replied the farmer. 'I think that pig's just got confused. His talent was too good to last.'

The villagers agreed. After three days, they stopped putting boards on the windows. They stopped closing the gates and putting the livestock in the barns and stoking their fires. That was a big mistake.

After seven days of haystack building, the pig's predication finally came true. A storm hit the village. It was ferocious, tearing through the little cobbled streets, pulling at the thatched roofs and howling through the doors, windows and chimneys. The old pig tucked himself down into the hay while the storm raged outside.

Farmer Carter and his wife dashed around the farm, pushing hard against the wind, soaked to the skin, as they tried to herd the pigs into the sties, hammer down the cold frame and greenhouse doors and board up the farmhouse windows. Eventually, they could do no more and retreated to the safety of the inglenook fireplace in the front room of the farmhouse.

The next day, the villagers emerged from their homes to look at the mess the storm had created. Straw from thatches was strewn across the streets, livestock were scared and sheltering under trees, the crops were flattened where they could not be harvested before the storm and the orchards were shaken to their very roots. They were dismayed, distraught and at a loss.

They gathered together to repair the damage and by the end of the day, the village was beginning to look a little better. The villagers had collected all the fallen fruit from the orchard and gathered in what crops they could, placing them all in the centre of the village. This way, they could share it out and nothing would go to waste – except, that was, for the plums. There were so many of them!

'What shall we do with them?' said the greengrocer. 'We can store the apples and the pears, but we cannot possibly eat all of these plums and they will not last!'

'Let's make a giant plum pudding!' said the baker.

That thought cheered the villagers and they wheeled the barrow of plums all the way to the bakery.

The farmer's pig awoke from the hay to the smell of fresh plum pudding cooking in the village. He loved plums, although Farmer Carter rarely let him near the orchard for just this reason. He hauled himself out of the hay and trotted out into the farmyard. The gate was open where the storm had damaged it and he walked through and followed the lane down into the village. There he found all the villagers seated around many tables in the village square, all tucking into hot plum pudding.

'Here!' shouted the blacksmith. 'Isn't that your weather pig, Carter?'

Farmer Carter turned to look. 'That it is!' he replied. 'He must have smelt the plum pudding.'

'Well he should have some!' said the baker. 'After all, he did try to warn us and we just didn't listen!'

'That's true,' Farmer Carter replied, laughing. He leant down and scratched the pig's head and the pig nuzzled up to the farmer, hopeful of plum pudding.

The baker served the pig a large slice of the pudding and the pig tucked in.

'From now on we shall call you Plum Pudding,' said Farmer Carter. 'A reminder of this day and never to ignore your hay stacking!'

And from that day on, the farmer's pig was indeed called Plum Pudding and the villagers never ignored the old pig's weather warnings again.

Activities

Whatever-the-Weather Adventures

The weather is changeable in April. One minute there's brilliant sunshine and the next, rain. There is an old country saying that goes 'don't shed your clout, 'til May is out'. Clout refers to your warm clothes, but the word 'May' does not refer to the month, it refers to the hawthorn flower, or mayflower. If it's a good year, the warm temperatures will bring the flowers out in April.

You don't have to wait for the mayflowers before you get out and about, though. As long as you've got a waterproof jacket, a hat or hood and a pair of wellington boots, you're ready for any adventure and here's some things you could do outside in April.

Just like Constance in 'A Land Without Snow', you could visit a park or public gardens where there are lots of cherry trees and make shapes in the blossom that has fallen beneath it. Use a stick to write your name in the blossom or make a 'snow' angel in it.

If it's been raining, pull on your welly boots and go puddle jumping. You could try making your very own puddle-o-meter on your boots by taping a bit of insulating tape vertically to the back of one of your boots. With a permanent marker, make centimetre marks on the tape to help measure the depth of your puddle. Now, stand in a puddle and see how deep it is with your puddle-o-meter. See who can jump in the deepest puddle!

If it's raining, why not make up your own rain dance. There are many cultures who have sung and danced to the rain to ask it to bless their crops. You could try turning some pots and pans upside down in your garden or porch and see what different sounds the rain makes on them. See if you can make up a tune or a song to go with them. And when you've finished singing and dancing, how about planting vegetable or flower seeds in the rain for that extra bit of rain magic to help them grow.

Rain Gauge and Windsock

Every day, we use complex technology and weather stations to predict what the weather is going to be, but we didn't always have this technology. Instead, people used weather lore and passed down knowledge from generation to generation. We still use some of these phrases today, such as 'red sky at night, shepherd's delight; red sky in the morning, shepherd's warning', 'clear moon, frost soon' and 'the higher the clouds, the finer the weather'.

There are ways we can measure the weather in our own back gardens, and the next activity shows how you can make a rain gauge to tell how much rain has fallen and a windsock to see which direction the wind is blowing in.

Once you've got your gauge and windsock set up, perhaps you will be able to see if, like in the story 'Stormy Weather', the wind is still cross with the rain or if they are finally working together?

Rain Gauge
You will need:

* masking tape
* ruler
* plastic fizzy drink or water bottle
* scissors
* felt tip pen

Take a clean, empty plastic bottle and cut it in two, around the circumference of the bottle, about a third from the top of the bottle and two-thirds from the bottom. Cut a piece of masking tape that is the length of the bottom two-thirds of the bottle and stick it vertically on the side of the bottle. Use the ruler to make marks 1cm apart along the tape with the felt tip pen.

Place the top third of the bottle upside down in the bottom third so that it becomes a funnel to catch the rain and prevents debris and small animals falling into the bottom of the bottle.

Find a place to put the gauge securely in your garden. You can do this by digging a hole in an empty bit of flowerbed or using a plant pot that is about 5cm deep and the same circumference as the bottle. Place the bottle in the hole or pot and push soil around it. Check the bottle each day to see how much rain has fallen. You could make a note in your Adventure Journal to observe the seasons and rainfall.

Windsock

You will need:

* small cardboard tube
* thin, coloured ribbons or coloured tissue paper
* stapler
* string
* garden cane.

Cut five lengths of different-coloured ribbon or tissue paper so that they are about 30cm long. Staple one end of each of the ribbons or tissue paper to the edge of one end of the cardboard tube.

On the other end of the tube, make three holes, an equal distance apart, around the edge.

Cut three pieces of string, around 12cm in length. Tie the end of one piece of string to one of the holes in the tube and repeat with the other three. Tie the other end of all three pieces of string together and then tie the strings to the top of a garden cane. Place the cane in the ground in the garden and watch the ribbons fly when the wind blows. Which direction is it blowing from?

Weather Collage

For this activity, you can create a rainbow just like Dämmerung's. Using tissue paper, you can create a collage on a sheet of blue paper and as you need sunshine *and* rain to make a rainbow, you could also place clouds on your picture using cotton wool. Have a go at creating different sorts of clouds by using the link to the cloud ID sheet in the back of the book.

You will need

* large sheet of blue paper
* tissue paper in all the colours of the rainbow
* cotton wool
* cloud-spotting guide (link to the Met Office guide in the back of the book)
* pencil
* glue.

To make the rainbow, start by drawing the outline of a rainbow on the sheet of paper. To do this, draw a large semi-circle and then draw a smaller one underneath. Tear up small pieces of the coloured tissue paper and fill the outline by sticking them onto the paper in colourful stripes that follow the semicircle, like a rainbow.

To create the clouds, look at the cloud ID sheet and see if you can recreate different clouds using cotton wool. Big fluffy cumulonimbus, thin stratus and wispy cirrostratus could all feature in different parts of your collage.

Plum Jam Pudding

Serves 6–8

In the story of 'The Weather Pig', after the storm, the villages have too many plums that have fallen off the trees and cannot store them, so they decide to make plum pudding. In this recipe, you can make your very own plum pudding using plum jam. Once you've made it, you could invite your friends over for a tea party, just like the village did, and then tell your friends the story of little Plum Pudding, 'The Weather Pig'.

Ingredients
115g butter
115g caster sugar
170g self-raising flour
2 eggs
a little milk
2 dessert spoons of plum jam

Method

* Grease the pudding basin well and place the plum jam in the bottom of the basin.
* Combine the sugar and the butter. Whisk the eggs and add them to the sugar and butter and fold in the flour.
* Mix all the ingredients together until you have a mixture with a soft dropping consistency. This means that when you hold a spoonful above the bowl, it drops slowly off the spoon back into the bowl. If the mixture is too stiff, add a little milk to get the consistency correct.
* Pour the mixture into the pudding basin on top of the jam. Cover the basin with baking parchment and secure with string or an elastic band. Place in a pan of water. The water should come halfway up the pudding basin. Place a lid on the pan, bring the water to the boil and then simmer for 1½ hours.
* To serve, let the pudding cool and then carefully remove the baking parchment, being aware the steam may escape from the basin and can burn you. Take a serving dish and place it on top of the basin. Hold the basin and plate firmly together and turn the whole thing upside down. Place them down on the side and lift the pudding basin off. Enjoy!

May

May bush flowers as the butterfly flits
And the early bird's chicks do fly
There's magic this month and the forest folk dance
Beneath the star-studded sky

The May Maze

Many say that spring is here when the hawthorn flower is blooming. Folk call it Mayflower, named after the month in which it blooms.

May is a magical month and hawthorn is a magical flower. There are many stories of folk who, when travelling the dusty roads, seek shelter under the hawthorn hedge, only to find themselves spirited away by the fairies and made to dance with them forever more. Yes, when you are near a hawthorn bush, you must be careful what you wish for, as one boy, a long, long time ago, found out.

Once upon a time, there was a boy who lived with his family in the middle of a forest. They lived a simple life, and he was loved, but the boy was always unsatisfied. He always wanted something more: the perfect rock to skim across the lake, the straightest arrow to hunt with or the smoothest wooden bowl to eat the ripest berries from. Nothing was ever quite good enough.

One day, he was walking in the forest collecting wood for the fire when he came upon a wall of thorny hedge studded with beautiful tiny white flowers. It stretched as far as he could see, to the right and the left. The boy stomped his foot. It would be a long walk around and he was very lazy.

He was about to turn for home when he noticed an opening in the hedge in front of him that had been camouflaged until then. Placing the wood he had collected at the bottom of the hedge, he stepped inside.

Inside were towering branches of the same hedge: thorny, dark and scattered with the tiny white stars of the hawthorn's flower. Just beside the doorway was a small wooden plaque that read: 'Enter to find your heart's desire.' So, the boy did.

Around the first corner he found a platter of round, rich, ripe fruits of the forest. Taking a blackberry from the top and squeezing it gently between his thumb and forefinger, he found it was plump and juicy and tasted as sweet as sweet could be. Next, he took a strawberry. He ate and ate until there was nothing left. He ate so much he fell asleep beneath the table and didn't wake until the sun was about to set.

Stretching his arms, he went to walk back through the maze of hedgerow but he couldn't find the entrance. Had it moved? He walked back and moved further on into the maze, searching for a way out. Soon, he found a soft feather bed with a duck-down duvet and so, realising he was tired, he settled himself on it for the night.

The next day he found all the pleasures he could wish for – fine wine, beautiful porcelain to eat from, handcrafted weapons with which to hunt for food and even a lake on which to skim the flattest of stones. This went on for many days.

His family were worried about where he had gone. They came searching for him many times, but they could not find him. You see, the magical maze only appears once a year in May and is invisible to all those who are happy with what they have. The boy couldn't hear their voices as they shouted for him and he was blissfully content within the maze with all his needs catered for.

A year passed and it was May again. The young boy started to feel an ache in his chest. He began to miss his mother's cooking and the conversations they would have at the dinner table. For all the riches he was presented with in the maze, he never once met a fellow human being. As the days passed, the more the ache grew, and the more he thought about how much he missed his family, until finally, he started to cry.

Instantly, a woman appeared before him. She was like nothing he had ever seen before and it was hard to look upon her without it hurting his eyes. She was as thin as the sharpest thorn on the hedge, as translucent as its green leaves and shimmered like the tiny white flowers. He could not decide if she was beautiful or frightening and his head hummed with too many thoughts.

'Why do you cry? Have I not provided you with every one of your heart's desires?' she asked.

'Yes,' sniffed the boy. 'Thank you,' he added.

'Then I ask again, why do you cry?'

'I miss my family, my mother's cooking, her wise words, my father's company and my sister's singing.'

'Ahh.'

'I'd give all of this up just to see them again.'

No sooner had he said it than he was back in the family home, with his mother standing by the stove, his father sewing a button onto his jacket and his sister singing as she washed the clothes. He hugged them all, and they were all overjoyed to see him once again.

'You look well,' his mother said, noticing his healthy waistline from the fine food he had indulged in.

'Not as well as I am now,' the boy replied. 'Never again will I wish for more than I need.'

He hugged his mother again, but he never told of where he had been. He knew the woman he had seen was a fairy, she could be nothing else, and he also knew that you should never, ever tell the secrets of the fairies.

The Glow-Worms and the Moon

By the roadside, if you look carefully, there is a thicket made of hawthorn and holly. It's not much to look at in the day but at night it is alight with tiny fires.

It wasn't always that way, though. You see, the little lights are glow-worms but the glow-worms that live in this thicket didn't always shine this brightly. There was a time when the glow-worms were just worms.

In the middle of the thicket, the worms would gather and start to spin their sticky threads on which to catch their dinner. It was dark in the thicket and only when the moon was at its fullest and most luminescent would the worms manage to catch enough to eat. On other nights, when the moon was only a fingernail of light in the sky, the worms did not do so well, and their bellies rumbled.

'Why does the moon not shine in full every night?' grumbled one worm.

'Does it not care that we are hungry?' griped another.

'The moon is very caring,' chimed in a small voice from the bottom of the hedge. It was Hedgehog, who had been sleeping soundly in the middle of the thicket and had been awoken by the worms' complaints.

'It doesn't feel that way,' grumped the biggest worm.

'Then why don't you ask her why?' replied Hedgehog.

'We will,' said the worms, together.

The next night the moon was full. The worms knew they had tiny voices and so they would have to join together for their calls to reach the moon.

'Moon! Moon!' they all called together.

The moon looked down at the trembling thicket full of little worms all shouting her name. She moved closer.

'Hello little worms.'

'We want to know why you cannot shine as bright every night?' the worms asked.

'I cannot shine every night, or I would become dull and fade to nothing,' replied the moon. 'I must rest, just as you sleep.'

'But you do sleep,' exclaimed the biggest worm, quite sure he was right. 'You sleep in the day when the sun comes out.'

'Oh no, little worm. I am still shining. I have other skies to light on the other side of the world.'

The worm thought hard. 'Could you not be a little less bright on other nights and then you would have enough shine for every night? Without your light, we cannot see to catch our food and when it's dark we are awfully hungry.'

The moon was caring, as Hedgehog had said, but she knew she must rest and recharge her moonlight. She could not shine brightly every night, so she thought for a while.

'I'll tell you what I'll do,' she said. 'I don't want you to go hungry and so I shall give you each a tiny speck of moon dust for the ends of your tails. You will be able to see to hunt by its fluorescent glow.'

The worms were overjoyed. Still to this day, so happy are they with the gift the moon has given them that every night they glow as brightly as they can, and if you listen very hard, they say a little thank you before going about their evening's work.

The Sprites of the Dingley Dell

Did you know that there are four different types of snake in the United Kingdom? They are adders, grass snakes, smooth snakes and barred grass snakes. None of them are dangerous if you leave them alone and keep a respectful distance, and the adder is the only one poisonous to humans.

Snakes hibernate from October to April but in May they come out to play. Most of the time you'll spot them basking in the sunshine and they will slither away if they hear your footsteps, but you might just be lucky enough to spot a grass snake swimming. They are excellent swimmers and like to eat small frogs, fish and birds. This story tells of a little grass snake that got a little bit greedy. Are you ready? Then I will begin.

Down in the Dingley Dell, where the water sprites played, lived a grass snake. It would spend its days beneath the waterfall listening to the laughing and splashing of the sprites. The snake had a good supply of frogs to eat beneath his rock, but everyone fancies a change every now and then and the snake thought the water sprites looked like a tasty meal.

Anyone who knows the water folk knows that sprites may look like they play all day and pay no attention, but in fact they see everything. They had seen the grass snake watching them, its scaly skin glistening, its tongue darting out from behind the flow of water tumbling over the rocks.

Sprites are light on their feet. They dance on the ripples of the woodland pools and the bubbles of the streams. The sprites jumped and hopped and danced and sang, always with one eye on the snake because they knew snakes could be tricksy.

The snake studied the sprites for many days, until finally it slid from the rock and dove under the water to fetch a different sort of meat for its dinner. They saw the snake as he slipped into the water and they whispered to each other a plan.

The snake circled below them, waiting for the perfect moment to strike. The sprites tripped, twirled and spun around and around. The snake followed their every move, until it saw its opportunity as one sprite danced a little further out than the others.

The snake lunged, aiming for the sprite's feet, but it couldn't get close enough. It was puzzled, and tried again and again, but it could not reach the sprite, no matter how hard it tried.

By now the snake could hear the sprites laughing. Looking over its shoulder, it tried to work out why it wasn't moving. Peering through the water, it saw what the problem was. As the snake had followed the sprites in their dance from its underwater vantage, they had led it around and around the winding willow roots, tying its body in a big knot around the roots.

'Help!' cried the snake. The more it tugged the tighter the knot got.

The sprites swam down to the snake keeping their distance as they circled it.

'We will help, but you must promise never to try and eat us again,' they said.

The snake agreed. It was happy to agree to anything, as it could not stay under the water for much longer, it needed to breathe.

The sprites freed the snake from the root, gently untying his body. It dashed off as soon as it was free, its pride dented. It swam to its rock and slid back underneath it, watching as the water folk resumed their dancing and their laughter at the snake's folly. Withdrawing further into the dark of the waterfall, the snake curled up on a damp ledge. Frogs didn't taste so bad after all, it thought. The snake had learnt its lesson and the sprites of the Dingley Dell were free to play once more.

The Halfway House

On the road to nowhere in particular, there is Halfway House that weary travellers may stop at. It is the house that holds the space between the faery lands and the human folk. To all it looks like a coaching inn with heavy, flint walls, a slate roof and stables to match but as the traveller rides through the carriage arch, they may find the walls of this world are more elastic than they thought.

One magical night, the night of the Beltane to be precise, a traveller named Rupert rode his horse through the arch, up to the stables of Halfway House and dismounted. Being a serious fellow, Rupert only believed in what he could see with his own eyes. He had travelled far and needed rest. Halfway House, with its bright flickering lights and gentle hum of voices emanating from it looked just the place.

Stabling his horse, he entered the tavern. The crackle of the fire chased away any last remnants of the cold, cloudless night outside and he walked towards the bar to order a drink and some food.

'Blessed be,' the landlord greeted Rupert.

'Blessed, indeed!' replied Rupert. 'Have you some warm food and a bed for the night?'

'Of course, although I warn you, there isn't much peace here at this time of year,' the landlord replied.

Rupert looked around the room. An old man sat by the fire warming his bones. On a long bench at the back of the room some farmers were talking, and a cat was curled up on a rocking chair purring.

'It looks perfectly peaceful to me,' Rupert replied.

'Oh it's not the earthly men you want to worry about,' said the landlord, lowering his voice. 'Tonight is the Beltane, the time when the faery folk come. It's a time when our worlds aren't so far apart.'

'Aye!' The old man spoke without looking up from the fire. 'Won't do you no harm, but they be noisy.'

Rupert laughed – faery folk indeed. 'I'll take my chances,' he said. 'What have you got to eat?'

'Wife's made a chicken broth and fresh bread, will that do?'

'More than do, thank you.'

Rupert took his meal and sat in the far corner of the tavern. His heavy eyelids battled with the hunger in his stomach and as soon as he'd eaten the warming broth and downed his sleep-inducing ale, he retired to his room for the night.

He fell asleep almost as soon as his head hit the pillow.

The night passed around him until he was woken, in the very early hours of the morning, by singing and music from the courtyard below. Unable to return to his slumber, he got up from his bed and walked to the window.

Rubbing his eyes, he pinched himself to see if he was awake. He was – but how could he be? What he saw below couldn't possibly exist.

There, in the courtyard, was the tavern owner and the old man, dancing and laughing with folk who looked like nothing of this earth: centaurs, half-man, half-horse; gamine faeries with translucent wings; prancing imps and elves with bells on their toes, and in the middle of them all was a maypole with a rainbow of ribbons around it and each dancer holding one of the ribbons. It was a sight to behold.

Rubbing his eyes again, he decided he must be dreaming and returned to his bed.

The next morning, the landlord greeted him again.

'I hope we didn't keep you awake last night,' he said. 'I don't bother to sleep on Beltane night. Can't beat them, join them, I say. They are friendly folk ,and they enjoy the mead and bread we make here.'

Rupert couldn't quite believe what he was hearing, 'Where are they from?'

'The wood, out back, yonder,' the landlord replied.

'I don't believe you. They were not of this Earth. I must have been dreaming. What was in that ale?' Rupert insisted.

'Suit yourself,' the landlord shrugged and went to make Rupert's breakfast.

But, you see, Rupert had made a mistake when he said the folk he had seen were not of this Earth. The woodland folk are of this Earth. Often, we just aren't looking hard enough to see them.

Activities

Hedgerow Stakeout

The hedgerow is alive at this time of year, full of animals and plants. For this month's adventure, let's go out and explore this habitat. It's time for a hedgerow stakeout; just make sure you watch out for fairies. Here's what you will need:

❋ suitable clothing in natural colours such as black, brown or green
❋ a foldable mat or blanket to sit on
❋ binoculars (optional)
❋ a drink and a snack
❋ your Adventure Journal.

Have a look on a map of the local area for the footpaths that are near you. See if you can find a field with a hedgerow that is near a footpath and that you can get to easily. Once you have decided which hedge to stake out, walk to it with your adult.

Next, you are going to want to find a comfy spot to sit where you can see the hedgerow and are sheltered from any sun, wind or potential rain. A tree is good for this or sit next to the hedge; hedges are great for shelter.

Check that where you are sitting isn't going to damage the hedgerow, is free of rubbish or dog doos and is not on private land. Place your sit mat or blanket down and make yourself comfortable. You are going to need to be as quiet as possible. When you first arrived, all the hedgerow animals will have spotted you and they will be hiding. Sit very quietly, and they will come back. Sit for as long as you can/want to and see what you can spot.

Here's what you might see:

Top of the hedge:
* elderflower
* hazel tree
* dunnock
* robin
* blackbird
* great tit
* spiders' webs
* glow-worms.

Middle of the hedge:
* hawthorn
* blackthorn
* orange tip butterfly
* painted lady butterfly
* large white butterfly
* comma butterfly
* sparrow
* wren
* holly.

Bottom of the hedge:

* bluebell
* dog violet
* stitchwort
* hedge mustard
* herb-robert
* nettles
* dock
* dandelion
* dormouse
* shrew
* field mouse
* beetle
* worm
* woodlouse.

When you have finished your stakeout, always leave the place as you found it and take any rubbish you have home with you. Don't forget, it's very bad luck to bring hawthorn flowers into the house, so however tempting it is to collect some of this magical flower, leave it in the hedgerow where it blooms, and if you do see a fairy, don't tell anyone.

The Lunar Cycle

Each month, the moon moves through eight phases. They are called the new moon, the waxing crescent, the first quarter, the waxing gibbous, the full moon, the waning gibbous, the third quarter and the waning crescent.

There are many stories of the moon and why it does this. Some myths tell of the moon being eaten by lions, wolves or dragons, and in the story of the glow-worms it is because the moon needs her rest.

The science is that it depends how much of the sun's light the moon's surface is reflecting and therefore how much of the moon's surface can be seen by us on Earth. Whatever part of the moon is reflecting the light, that is what we can see.

For this activity, we will be observing all these stages. Here's what you will need:

* your Adventure Journal
* a pen or pencil
* a digital or polaroid camera.

Start when you know there is going to be a new moon. That means you can only see a very faint outline of the moon and it looks completely black. You can find a calendar of the moon's phases on the Time and Date website. There is a link to this in the back of the book.

Observe the moon during each of its different phases; there is a different phase approximately every four days. Draw the moon or take a picture of it and stick in it your Adventure Journal. Write a bit about what it looks like and how it makes you feel. Soon, you'll have your very own moon story.

Pause as the Wheel Turns

Beltane

Easily one of the most well-known festivals in the wheel of the year, many people celebrate Beltane on the first weekend in May, but traditionally it's May's eve, 30 April to 1 May. On Beltane night, two fires called balefires were lit and danced around with glee. A path was cleared between the two fires and livestock – cows, sheep, horses and goats – were walked between them for protection and to bestow blessings for the coming year. Perhaps this was because the heat and smoke from the fires cleared the animals' hides of any bugs and parasites that might be inhabiting them – either way, this tradition was carried out every year as part of the farming calendar.

Beltane is a night for celebration; a night to feast on food, safe in the knowledge that the summer will bring plenty. It's also when that liminal space, that space you can only see if you squint, the space between this world and the fairy world, is thin.

This is a time when the fairies can cross over and dance with us, but be careful not to wander into their world, for if you hear their music or eat their fairy food, you will not be able to resist and you may well stay there for longer than you anticipated. A minute in their world may be a decade in ours. If you do stray into the world of the fae, be sure to treat them with respect, keep your promises and never speak of their world in this one.

Beltane Crown

If you are going to dance with the fairies on Beltane night, you are going to want to make sure you are properly dressed for the occasion. A crown is a great place to start, as circles in many cultures represent the cycle of life, fertility and good luck.

I have suggested using wool to make a plait as the base of your crown. You can use different-coloured wool to represent a maypole or you could use green wool to represent a snake, like the one in the story of the sprites of the Dingley Dell.

In Norse mythology, snakes are a symbol of strength and guardianship. For example, *Jörmungandr* could be seen as fulfilling this role as the Midgard serpent, wrapped around the worlds. To the Greeks, the snake can also be a symbol of knowledge and fertility and for the Aborigines, their creation story tells of the Rainbow Snake, who is responsible for water, life, fertility and abundance.

You will need:
* tape measure
* chunky wool in a colours of your choosing
* scissors
* flowers from the garden or a bunch from the local shop.

To make:
Measure your head by putting the tape measure around the circumference of your head just above your ears. Make a note of the circumference and add 15cm, as this is the length you will need to make your plait to fit around your head and extra for tying a bow to keep it in place. Make a note of this measurement.

Try to choose chunky wool for this project or you could double up with thinner wool. Use the measurement you made of your head plus the extra and cut three pieces of the wool all the same length. Tie the end of all three pieces of wool together in a knot. Secure the knotted end to a flat surface with some sticky tape. Now, plait the wool and tie it into a knot at the end once you have finished. Put the plait around your head, tying the two ends in a knot or bow. Take the plait off. You should now have a circle shape.

Take your flowers and weave the stems into the plait. Now place the plait back on your head and you should have a Beltane crown!

Rainbow Salad

The maypole that is danced around on Beltane night has a rainbow of ribbons and in this recipe, you get to create your own rainbow and explore different foods together. You can make this recipe for however many you like, with whatever ingredients you like. Below are some suggestions.

Ingredients
Red:
red pepper, tomatoes, radishes, red oak lettuce, pomegranate seeds

Orange:
carrots, orange pepper, roasted sweet potato, oranges, mango

Yellow:
spring onions, cheese, yellow pepper, banana, sweet corn, cooked couscous or pasta

Green:
spinach, pea shoots, lettuce, cucumber, bean shoots, avocado

Purple:
red cabbage, cooked purple sprouting broccoli, heritage purple carrots, red onion

Method
* Take your chosen salad ingredients and prepare them. Cook them if needed, wash and peel.
* Have fun – for example, make stars with the cucumber, grate the carrot and mix couscous with spring onion and sweetcorn.
* Once you have your five different colours of ingredients prepared, take a plate and start arranging them in a semi-circle like a rainbow – red at the top, next orange, then yellow, then green and lastly purple.
* Enjoy!

June

Dog roses bloom and wild strawberries ramble
Along the hedgerowed trails.
Take your time to saunter and amble
While the sky above fills with forked tails

Race to the Sun

The birds of summer are a sight to behold! On sunny days, the sky is filled with forked-tail beings, on a roller coaster of clouds and heatwaves.

Look up, and high above the pavement, on the telephone wire, there sit three birds: a house martin, a swallow and a swift. They are cousins, and yet each is a little different. The house martin has a white band on her tail, the swallow has a dab of red beneath his throat, and the only white on the swift is a spot below her chin. Today they are arguing.

'We are the fastest by far,' insists house martin.

'No. We are faster,' replies the swallow.

'Nonsense, it is the swifts who are fastest, it's in our name!'

'Why don't you settle it with a race,' says Yaffle, the green woodpecker, who has been listening to the argument and sees an opportunity.

'Done!' reply the three birds, in unison at last.

'Once around the sun and back,' announces the woodpecker, knowing full well they will never reach it. You see, he knows that while the three birds are gone, all the tastiest bugs will be his for the taking. He hammers on the telegraph pole and the race begins.

The house martin is the first to falter. After several miles she still isn't getting any closer to the sun and suspects that Yaffle has tricked them. She knows the woodpecker is greedy and that he must be after the best bugs. If the woodpecker eats them all there will be none for her babies.

Returning to the earth, she catches Yaffle snaffling all the bugs.

'You tricked us!' she says.

'You wanted a race,' laughs Yaffle, his mouth full.

The swallow has seen the house martin return and begins to have his own suspicions about Yaffle, so he too flies back to confront the naughty woodpecker.

Together the house martin and swallow chase the woodpecker back into the woods before going back to find the swift. Looking up, they can see her high above them and they worry that she has become lost.

They shout to her, 'Swift! Swift! Come back, the woodpecker tricked us!'

'No,' sings the swift.

'But you'll never reach the sun,' the two other birds twitch and twitter. 'It's too dangerous, we'll concede, you're the fastest!'

'I'm having too much fun to come down!' shouts the swift.

The swift flies on through the clouds and around the burning sun star.

On the way back, she shrieks all the way of how she has flown around the sun. Of course, the other birds don't believe she actually reached it, but the little swift doesn't care – and that is why you will always hear swifts screeching in the summer. Listen closely, and they'll tell you of their journeys.

The Mole Who Loved the Sun

It is well known that moles cannot see very well, but what's not so widely known is how that came about.

In the first garden the world ever knew, there was a grapevine. It grew on a southerly rockface, winding its way up the stones, grasping the rough edges, curling its shoots around the granite and finally, at the very, very top, it almost reached the sun. At the bottom of the vine there lived a mole.

It was the longest day of the year, the summer solstice, the day the animals celebrated because the light lasted longer than on any other day. After a long day of digging, the mole brushed the soil from his eyes with his aching claws and sighed.

'How I would love to be able to see the sun. I spend all day underground and then by the time I get to rest the sun is so high I cannot see her.'

'I'll help you,' came a little voice from beside him in the mud. It was a little yellow and black caterpillar and he grinned at Mole. 'I'll take the message to the top of the vine and there I will speak to the sun for you.'

'Oh would you?' said Mole

'Of course,' Caterpillar replied, and began the long journey.

Mole waited patiently below, watching the caterpillar as he wriggled his way up the vine. Soon he was out of sight and all Mole could do was wait.

After half an hour of climbing, Caterpillar stopped to snack on some grapes. He was very hungry. He ate and ate until his tummy started to feel very funny. An overwhelming tiredness came upon him and his body started to feel stiff and achy.

Blackbird swooped down to pluck Caterpillar from the vine, but Caterpillar cried out, 'Please don't, I have an important message for the sun.'

'You'll never make it to the top,' said Blackbird, looking more closely at the caterpillar, who had started to grow a little leather jacket. 'It looks like you're making a chrysalis and you'll need your rest to become a butterfly, I'll take the message for you.'

'Oh, thank you,' said Caterpillar, who was feeling rather uncomfortable now. 'Just tell me the message and I'll fly up to the sun.'

'Mole would love to see the sun.'

What an odd message thought Blackbird, but she had promised and so off she went. Following the vine upwards, she beat her wings and travelled the journey she had made many times before, for her nest was in the vine. As she passed her nest, her little ones shouted out to her. 'We're hungry, please feed us!'

She stopped. 'I have an important message to deliver, I will be back with food soon.'

'But we're hungry!'

Now Squirrel heard the commotion and, knowing what it was like to have young ones at home, he offered to help. 'I'll take the message for you,' he said.

'Oh, would you?' Blackbird replied, gratefully. 'It's a very simple message. Mole loves the sun.'

'How very strange,' said Squirrel.

'I know,' said Blackbird, 'but there it is!'

Squirrel nodded and ran fast up the branches of the vine and as they thinned towards the top his nimble feet skipped from limb to limb, balancing on the fresh grapes and the spiralling tendrils. When he got to the top, he shouted out to the sun. 'Sun! Sun! Before you climb any higher, I have an important message for you.'

Now, before you worry, Squirrel was careful not to look at the sun for he knew the great power the sun held.

'A message for me?' replied Sun.

'Yes. Mole is in love with you.'

'With me?' Well, the sun was overjoyed. She'd never heard anyone say they loved her before. Of course, they loved her warmth, her rays, the life she gave them, but no one had actually said they loved her! 'I must go and see him at once.'

Sun slipped from the sky, leaving trails of red, orange, pink and lilac behind her and as she got closer and closer, she could see Mole below looking up at her waiting for her to arrive. Sun arrived on the earth and the sky became darker and darker. Mole squinted at the bright glow glinting on the earth.

'Sun, is that you?'

'It is,' Sun replied.

But Mole did not know the power the sun held, and as he looked at her his vision started to fade until he could see almost nothing. He did not realise that by looking straight at her, he would never be able to see anything clearly again.

'I cannot see you, you are just a faint glow.'

'I am sorry Mole,' replied the sun. 'You should not have looked straight at me, I am so bright I have damaged your eyes.'

'It was worth it, to see your beauty, even if it was only a glimpse', said Mole.

And the sun smiled. No one had loved her this much before. 'I will visit you every day,' she promised, 'so you can feel the warmth of my rays.'

'I would like that very much,' replied Mole.

And this is why the mole does not see very well, and why the sun sets every night.

The Golden Hawkmoth

Hawkmoths are one of the biggest moths in the United Kingdom. You'll often find they are named after other animals too. The bee hawkmoth, hummingbird hawkmoth and the elephant hawkmoth are good examples.

This story is about hummingbird hawkmoth. These moths are about 5cm in size, and they hover next to flowers to sup the pollen with their long tongue called a proboscis. They look a lot like a miniature hummingbird, hence their name.

Harry was a hummingbird hawkmoth who loved to drink the sap of the pine tree. It wasn't sweet like the pollen the other moths craved, it was sour, and Harry loved its taste. The energy it gave him meant he could drum his wings faster than any other moth. It was tricky to get to and he had to use his tiny proboscis to work away at the bark and get to the sweet, sticky sap. It meant he was always on the move, busy gathering the next mouthful.

The other hawkmoths warned him that he would regret his love of the pine tree sap. Sap was not for a hawkmoth. The nectar of flowers was more than enough. They said he needed to rest and his constant search for the pine tree sap would one day be his downfall.

But Harry didn't care. He kept going day after day, night after night, flitting this way and that among the woodland that was his home. The white lilies, tiny blue pansies and bright red poppies held no interest for him.

After a particularly satisfying meal, Harry was about to head on to the next tree when he spotted a tiny jewel of sap on the end of his proboscis. He tried to suck it up, but it was stuck fast. It was a hard resin, it wasn't moving.

He asked the other moths what it was, and they explained that when the sap of the pine tree dries, it goes hard. He must be careful not to get it on his wings or face as it would stick fast. Harry looked back at his wings and fluttered them as fast as he could. He could see tiny sparkling drops of hard resin, catching in the sunlight.

'I'm not worried,' laughed Harry. 'The sap adds even more beauty to my wings. Now I am the fastest and the most beautiful hawkmoth in the wood.'

The other hawkmoths shook their heads. They feared for Harry, but he would not listen.

After months of gathering sap from the pine trees, Harry had a crown of golden sap shards on his head. It slowed him down but not enough. The years rolled on and the resin soon coated every part of Harry, all but his wings. That was because they were constantly moving and the resin didn't have time to set, although it wasn't long before the weight of the resin slowed him down.

Early one morning, when the moon was still in the sky as it sometimes is, Harry came to rest on the stump of a fallen pine tree. It was the first time he had stopped in over a decade. As he tried to preen the dried sap from his wings the other moths watched on in dismay. Some even tried to help, but as the moon disappeared and the sun crept higher and higher, the rays of its light reached Harry and started to dry the resin.

Soon he could not move his wings and eventually he stood stock still, never to move again. He became the perfect golden statue of a hawkmoth. The other moths could do nothing.

Harry still stands on the stump, to this day, and the other moths, who are not without compassion, visit him. Older moths who remember Harry the restless hawkmoth tell his story to the younger moths, who listen in awe, remembering the harsh lesson Harry learnt.

Next time you are in a pinewood, see if you can find the statue of Harry the golden hawkmoth, sitting on his pine tree stump.

Roma

Once upon a time, there were three chickens living on a hill in the country. One was named Stayput, one was named Comfort and one was named Roma. One chicken stayed where she was, next to the big apple tree, pecking at the food she found closest to it, the second slept on the same familiar branch of the tree each night and the third liked to adventure far and wide, explore the world and find new friends. Can you guess which one was which?

After a long, hot summer, the day came when the grass no longer grew around the tree. Stayput had eaten it all and there had been no rain for months. Comfort could not roost happily on her branch because all the leaves of the tree had curled up into sharp lumpy bumpy nobbles in the drought. The only hen who knew what to do was Roma – they had to move on.

'I don't want to move,' said Stayput.

'I like my comfortable branch,' said Comfort.

'But we have no water,' replied Roma. 'All you have to do is follow me and I will show you where there is water and a warm barn for shelter. There's even a little patch of wild strawberries nearby.'

'But we like it here!' said Stayput and Comfort, stubbornly.

Now, Roma had been out exploring many times and had found the barn she talked about. It was just over the hill, lined with hay and it had a stream running right next to it that watered the wild strawberries and kept them fresh. She could have left the other two hens and gone there on her own, but Roma was a kind hen and didn't want Stayput and Comfort to suffer when she knew there was a life of luxury so close. She just had to get them to see it.

The days wore on and so did the drought. Roma spent her days at the barn eating corn and strawberries and drinking water from the stream, but she returned at dusk every day to try to persuade her sisters to join her. Stayput and Comfort still would not move, and their empty tummies rumbled louder each day.

'We're hungry!' they complained to Roma.

And then Roma had an idea. 'I'll go and get us some food!' she said.

Running all the way to the barn, Roma gathered enough strawberries for the two hungry hens. Hurrying back, she dropped two at Stayput and Roma's feet. They gobbled them up and looked for more. Roma dropped another strawberry on the ground, moving a little further away from the tree each time.

Roma kept dropping the strawberries and Stayput and Comfort kept eating them. They were so hungry that they didn't look up. They didn't realise they'd walked far, far away from the tree, Stayput's patch of stubbly grass and Comfort's branch. Instead, they were standing in a barn that was warm and lined with hay. The loft space was perfect for roosting and they could hear a little stream outside that would provide them with water.

As Roma laid the last strawberries on the ground, the other two hens looked up at the rafters of the barn.

'Wow!' said Stayput.

'It's a castle,' said Comfort.

'Isn't it wondeful?' replied Roma, bursting with pride at the place she had found them. She was relieved that she had finally managed to get the silly hens to move.

'Why didn't you tell us about this place?' Stayput and Comfort asked.

Roma shook her head and watched, smiling, as the other two hens ran off around the barn busying themselves gathering straw to make comfortable beds. They hadn't even thanked her, but she didn't care. They were all together and safe. This barn was indeed a castle, and they would live in comfort for the rest of their lives.

Activities

Swift Spotting in the Meadow

Swifts start to arrive in mid-spring in the UK. They travel here from the Sahara, where they have been taking their winter holiday. With strong scythe-shaped wings, swifts nock themselves to the air currents and fly like arrows across the ocean. For many, swifts are the first sign of summer's arrival. Their shrieking cries and thrill-seeking dives make them a fabulous bird to watch.

For this activity, you will need to find a field or open green space and choose a warm day. The swifts catch the little bugs that fly above the fields at this time of year and so a field with sheep in it is a great place to swift spot, but you must check you are allowed to enter the field before you do.

You don't need a lot for this activity, in fact, you could just use the naked eye to spot the swifts as you should be able to tell it's them from the shrieking call they make, but if you want to be really sure then take a pair of binoculars and a good bird guide.

There are two other birds that look a lot like swifts from a distance. They are swallows and house martins. Here's a quick guide on what they look like:

Swift:
* dark brown to black feathers
* pale throat and sometimes forehead
* forked tail, often closed when flying
* loud, shrill, almost screaming call.

Swallow:
* black feathers with blue towards the tops of the wings and head
* distinctive red throat
* white feathers across its belly
* the biggest of the three birds

House martin:
* black feathers with blue towards the tops of the wings and head
* bright white throat, belly and rear where its tail feathers join its body
* smaller than a swallow and a swift.

If you don't have a bird guide, before you go out try looking these birds up on the internet. Study the pictures of them to help you to remember what you are looking for.

Once you have a suitable open space, make sure you are dressed appropriately for the weather and have sunscreen on, and then all there is left to do is to wait and see if you can spot the swifts of summer. Listen for them shrieking and screeching about their journeys.

In your Adventure Journal, why not try and write your own story of the swift's journey from the Sahara? What animals did she see on the way? What did the lands that she flew over look like? Do you think she saw a whale as she flew over the ocean?

If you spot the first swift arriving and the last swift leaving, you can record this online with the Woodland Trust or the RSPB. The best time to spot them is early morning or as the sun is setting.

Pause as the Wheel Turns

Litha

Midsummer is almost here, and 21 June is traditionally referred to as the summer solstice, the longest day of the year. In the wheel of the year this festival, or sabbat, is known as Litha.

This is the month when the rose bushes are coming into bloom, a time when the fire spirit is ever present in the glorious sun, and the earth is full of life and basking in its rays. The Oak King and the Holly King prepare to do battle, once more, for the light and dark halves of the year. It's time to pause, go outside and take in the beauty of summer.

Sit on your patio, make yourself a cup of herbal tea, light a candle – red, orange or yellow are good for this time of year – and watch the sun go down or indulge in a spot of fairy watching in the twilight. Decorate the house with summer flowers and sweep out the hearth in honour of the fire spirits. It's the perfect time for a family trip out to visit a public garden, a stone circle like Avebury or Stonehenge, or an Iron Age fort, maybe Figsbury Ring and Danebury Ring. There are many magical places.

Solstice Vine Party

This activity is great for the back garden, but you can also use a balcony or an area in your house if you do not have a garden.

What you will need:
* washing line or string
* green wool or ribbons
* pictures of the animals featured in the 'The Mole Who Loved the Sun' and other animals who may live in the vine, for example, garden birds, butterflies, mini beasts, snakes and lizards, either drawn by you or printed out from the internet
* glue

Let your imagination go wild for this activity. Find a suitable spot to hang your washing line or string, ensuring that either end is secure. If you have a permanent washing line, you could use that where it is and it doesn't matter what sort it is, as long as it has string or line to hang things on.

Take lengths of the green wool or ribbon and tie them to the washing line so that they hang vertically from the line. Once you have a jungle of green, now you can add your art. Cut out your drawings and use a small dab of glue to stick the animals at the appropriate height in the vines. Mini beasts might crawl around at the bottom, lizards in among the vines, while butterflies and birds fly high at the top.

When you've finished, try recreating the story of the 'The Mole Who Loved the Sun'. Why not invite some friends around and have a summer solstice tea party, make the summer pudding recipe below, and play a game of Whispered Messages …

Whispered Messages

To play this, sit in a circle with your friends. Think of a message you would like to pass up the vine, just like Mole did. Whisper it to the friend on your right. They then whisper it to the friend on their right, and so on, until it goes around the whole circle. Once the message has been passed around everyone in the circle, see if the message the last person heard is the one you told the first person.

Clay Creatures

What you will need:
* air-drying modelling clay
* gold paint.

For this activity, you will need to look up some pictures of hawk moths as a reference. There are lots of lovely photos on the UK Moths website and there's a website link in the back of the book to help you find them.

When you have your reference material, you can use the air-drying modelling clay to create your version of the Golden Hawkmoth. Follow the instructions on the clay packet to get the best results. You could even try making a tree stump for the moth to sit on.

Once your model is dry, paint it with gold paint so you have your very own Golden Hawkmoth.

Strawberry Summer Pudding

Serves 6–8

Roma, Comfort and Stayput loved strawberries and you're going to need lots for this fruity summer recipe. You can use fresh or frozen, and here's how to make your summer pudding.

Ingredients

8–10 slices of bread with the crusts removed
900g fresh summer fruits – blackcurrants, redcurrants, raspberries, blueberries, strawberries
150g caster sugar

Method

❋ Place the sugar in a saucepan with 4 tbsp of water. Heat gently until dissolved. Add the harder summer fruits (redcurrants, blackcurrants, plums) to the pan and simmer until soft. Then add the softer fruit (strawberries, raspberries, blueberries) for just a couple of minutes at the end.

❋ Remove from the heat.

❋ Line the sides and base of a 1.25 litre pudding basin with the bread, moulding the bread to the bowl and leaving no gaps in the bread. Reserve a couple of slices for the lid.

❋ Pour the stewed fruit into the bread-lined bowl, keeping back a few tablespoons of the stewed fruit juice. Add the reserved bread to the top of the bowl and pour the remaining juice over it.

❋ Place a plate on top of the basin that's approximately the same size as the basin and weight it down. Leave in the fridge overnight, turn out onto a dish and serve.

July

A trip to the coast is what I love the most
Where the sea creatures duck and dive
Here from the shore, I watch seabirds soar
And crabs wave their claws at the tide

A New Home for Herman

There once was a little hermit crab whose dreams were big. Each year, he moved to a new shell but each year, he wanted something a little bigger; a little more luxurious and a little more in keeping with his station in life, which he believed was well above that of your average hermit crab. Or at least, that's what Herman thought. No winkle, whelk or top shell, however painted, was good enough for Herman. He dreamed of the conch shells his cousins enjoyed in the Caribbean. The problem was Herman was never going to find one of those on his beach.

On a particularly sunny day, Herman was wandering the beach looking for a new home. 'Something with status,' he thought. 'Something grand!' And then he saw it.

Haloed in the sun's rays, the most glorious palace he had ever seen.

'That's it!' Herman announced, and scuttled over to it. It was a castle in the sand, edged with scallops and cockles. The turrets were perfection and the crenulations exquisite.

'This shall be my new home,' he said, and moved in immediately, discarding his old shell by the front door.

The sun arced across the sky and the tide began to turn, moving slowly across the beach. It edged closer and closer to Herman's new home. Herman was sleeping soundly inside and did not hear the crashing waves or the rush of the water as it pooled around the sand castle, washing away the foundations.

Within hours, Herman's new house was surrounded, and he awoke to find his claws in salty water and the walls of his house full of holes. Time wore on and so did the sea. By midnight, Herman's magnificent castle was underwater.

Sighing, Herman turned to find his old house, the whelk shell he'd left by the front door of the castle, but it had been washed away. All he could find was a winkle shell. Herman crawled in and waited for the tide to turn.

Finally, when the sun rose again and the sand was once more exposed, Herman started his hunt for a new house. The winkle shell was nowhere near as comfortable as his dog whelk shell and Herman was miserable. He had been silly to give up his shell so easily and this time, as he searched, he remembered that castles aren't always what they appear to be.

How the Whale got his Barnacles

Once upon a time, there was a great big blue whale. He was the envy of all the other sea creatures with his huge swishing tail, crashing and splashing in the sea. Fish would come from all around for rides on the showers of seawater he spouted from the top of his head. It was a happy life.

But at some point in our lives, we will all want something we cannot have, and the whale was no different. He longed to walk on the land and discover the mountains that reached out of the sea, high up into the sky.

'Go to the rock pools,' said the fish, 'There are many things with legs there. Perhaps they will tell you how to grow them.'

A good idea, thought the whale, and off he went.

Now, when the tide is high, the whale easily reaches the rock pools. He has no trouble swimming to them but, on this occasion, the tide was too high, and the whale was too big. He could not get down under the rocks to the tiny crabs and shrimps he wanted to talk to. He had to wait.

He waited and waited and finally the tide was just low enough. The first creature he saw was a tiny hermit crab scuttling along the bottom of the pool.

'Stop, stop,' said the whale. 'I need to know how to grow legs.'

'I have no idea,' said the hermit crab. 'I know how to find a new home. Ask the shrimp, he has many legs.'

It wasn't long before the whale spotted a shrimp.

'Shrimp, shrimp,' said the whale. 'How can I grow legs?'

'I'm not sure,' said the shrimp. 'If I lose a leg, it just grows back. I do not know how though. Ask the starfish. He has five strong legs.'

And so the whale asked the starfish.

'I too can grow my legs back if I lose them, but you have to be born with them,' said the wise old starfish.

The whale sighed. Not one of these creatures could tell him how to grow legs. Even worse, the tide was so far out that the whale was stuck in the rock pool. The sun was starting to burn the whale's back and he was getting very uncomfortable. He wiggled and squiggled to try and push himself off the rocks but he wasn't getting anywhere.

'Help! Help!' cried the whale. 'I'm stuck.'

'We can help,' the barnacles sang from the rocks surrounding him.

'How can you help me?' sobbed the whale. 'You are so tiny and you have no legs at all.'

'But we have strong feet and there are many of us. We can push you back into the water.'

'Oh, would you? Please do,' said the whale, who was now desperate to get back to the salty depths of the ocean.

The barnacles grouped together and pushed hard against the side of the whale. 'Heave ho!' they shouted. 'Heave ho!'

He was free in no time, swimming back to the sea.

'Thank you,' said the whale, looking back and seeing the barnacles still attached to his sides. 'There's no need to stay, you can go back to the rocks now.'

'But we can't,' squeaked the barnacles. 'With no fins or tails, we cannot swim back to the rock pool. Please let us stay.'

Well, how could the whale say no? The barnacles had saved his life. And so it was that the whale did not get his legs but instead he had the many feet of the barnacles that now remained with him. He swam back to his home, happy that he was safe and he had found so many new friends. If you look, many whales have barnacles attached to them, perhaps this is why?

Special Delivery

In the dark depths of the ocean lives a creature called a nautilus. It is a strange-looking animal that has been around for millions of years. A magnificent shell – white, with rusty red stripes – houses many long tentacles that protrude from it and help the nautilus to propel itself through the water. The really wonderful thing about a nautilus is that it can draw water into its shell and use it to move up or down in the sea. If it really wants to, it can travel all the way to the surface of the ocean and greet the white tops of the waves.

A lot of people know all of this about the nautilus, but what they don't know is that it has a very special job in the ocean. It is a messenger for all the sea creatures. The nautilus can take messages from the sharks swimming below to the dolphins riding the breakers; from the anglerfish in the dark depths to the seals swimming through the waves.

This story is about Neville, an apprentice nautilus. It takes a nautilus approximately two years to complete his or her messenger training and once they have finished, they are authorised to deliver messages anywhere in the ocean. The most promising trainees are selected to become a King's Messenger; messengers for Neptune himself.

Neville was an outstanding pupil, conscientious and hardworking, but he was bored with relaying the little messages: the whispers between the cockles and the clams, the meetings between the starfish and the buzz among the coral. He wanted to travel the oceans, talk to great white sharks, humpback whales and walruses, but that would not be allowed until he had completed his training. As I said, he was already well ahead of the other little nautili but he was still only a year through his training and he wasn't very gracious about it.

'I should be an official messenger by now,' Neville grumbled. 'I'm as good as you,' he said, one day, to his tutor.

'Patience, Neville,' his tutor replied.

His tutor knew Neville wasn't a bad nautilus and could see that he was bored. He wanted to find a way to help Neville, so he decided to visit Neptune and ask if Neville could become an apprentice with the King's Messengers. Neptune agreed, on the condition that Neville passed his test. Neville would have to deliver a message from the smallest creature at the bottom of the ocean to the tiniest creature at the top.

The next day Neville was bobbing along with his friend Nora, waiting for his next assignment, when a tiny shrimp scooted up to him. 'I have an urgent message,' stuttered the shrimp, breathless and in a bit of a tizzy. Can you go to the top of the ocean and tell the krill I need them to come and clean the plankton from my little house. It's getting very green in there and it's clashing with my lovely corals.'

Neville started to laugh. 'I'm far too busy for that. You could clean your own walls easily enough, you're a shrimp, aren't you?' Neville jetted water from his shell and bobbed away.

Nora had also heard the shrimp. She too was a trainee messenger. 'I'll go for you, if you'd like?' she offered. She knew it would be a long way, she wasn't as big as Neville and it would be hard work, but she wasn't afraid of a challenge.

'Oh, would you?' The little shrimp hugged her gratefully.

'I'll be as quick as I can.'

Nora pushed water from her shell and travelled up and up, past the lobsters on the sandy ledge, past the dolphins playing in the currents and past the cod gossiping by the trawler net. Her tentacles started to ache as she dodged the seagulls skewering fish towards the surface, but she pushed on knowing the shrimp had been in ever such a state and once she had delivered her message she could rest.

Finally, she reached the krill. Panting a little from the journey, she passed on the message and no sooner had she done so than King Neptune appeared. Nora was so tired she didn't have the puff to even bob a little bow, but King Neptune didn't mind.

'Nora,' he said, lowering his usually booming voice so as not to scare the little nautilus. 'You are a truly a worthy messenger. Would you like to become an apprentice with the King's Messengers?'

'Your majesty …' was all that Nora could muster and she gathered her puff together and bobbed a bow. It was a great privilege and she couldn't wait to get started.

Further down the sea, Neville heard of Nora's apprenticeship and grumbled. 'It should have been me.'

'And it would have been,' replied his tutor, 'if you had just delivered the message. That is our job, after all. You have much to learn, Neville. The messages from the shrimp are just as important as those from the great white shark. Perhaps now you will be a little more humble.'

Neville thought about what his tutor had said and after his day of messaging, instead of rushing off to play with his friends, he went to the little shrimp's house to apologise and offered to help him clean his house. He used his tentacles to reach the bits of plankton the krill had not been able to and chatted to the little shrimp as he worked.

To this day, Neville and the little shrimp are good friends. Neville never became a King's Messenger. Instead, he is content to bob with the shrimp and gossip with the cockles. He keeps his ear close to the ground, never misses a message and he is known throughout the ocean as one of the most reliable messengers you can find.

The Five Shore-Gulls

In a seaside town, not too far from here, live five seagulls. They have been together since they were born, they were raised in the same nest. They feast on the food the human tourists leave scattered about – chips, hotdogs, candy floss and ice cream – but of all the human delicacies they love the most, they love doughnuts.

Now they are fully grown, these gulls have forgotten the sea. They had watched the day that their mother and father had flown away across the breaking surf and into the distance. They had watched as the tiny dots disappeared into the clouds on the horizon and they had simply shrugged. They had not mourned their loss or even thought to follow.

They had heard of the trawler ships they could follow for fish and the food that could be found at sea, but they were 'shore-gulls' now, they laughed, not seagulls. Besides, there was a plentiful supply of food along the seaside boulevard. The lingering smell of hot, sugared dough held them captive and if the humans would not give up their bounty willingly then the brothers would simply take it from their hands. The shrieks and waving arms only delighted them further.

On a particularly sunny day in the height of summer, when the pier was packed with people and food, noise and lights, the gulls spotted their favourite dish: hot doughnuts. A small child was clutching a large bag of the sugary treats and the gulls knew that this was fair game.

The biggest one flew down to grab the bag, as he always did, while the other brothers flew around the child to distract them. But as the brother grasped the bag with his feet, the child held tight. She was not letting go of her bounty. The bag started to slip from her hands, and she dug her heals into the pier.

The other brothers started to pull at her hair, but she was not to be put off. No gull was going to part her from her doughnuts, her yearly holiday treat! Her parents shouted at her to let go of the bag as she moved further and further towards the railings that lined the edge of the pier.

The seagulls all pulled, and the surf below roared. Just as she was about the hit the railing, her father lifted her up out of harm's way and the seagulls gained their prize.

But the brother with the bag didn't have a good grip and at the suddenness with which he won the doughnuts, he dropped them into the sea below the pier.

The doughnuts started to drift out to sea and the brothers flew down to retrieve them. Now a floating mass of hot sticky dough and seagull's feathers, the brothers feasted on the floating treasure.

The sea was rough that day and the wind strong. It wasn't long before the gulls were far out to sea and the doughnuts were finished. As the older brother looked up, all he could see about him was water – endless, rolling, salty water.

'We're lost!' he squawked.

'No, we're not,' said another.

'We'll fly to the shore,' a third replied.

'Where is the shore?' exclaimed a fourth.

The talking and squawking went on until there was such a cacophony coming from the birds that it brought the attention of an old albatross. A huge bird with a wingspan of twelve feet wide, the albatross is often called the old man of the sea. They can fly for miles and miles and they love to follow the fishing trawlers to gather their food.

'Look, there's a Mollymawk!' shouted one of the brothers.

Now, what you need to know, reader, is that Mollymawk is not a polite name for an albatross. It means 'stupid gull' and the brother seagulls did indeed think that the albatross was stupid, for they had heard how he spent long days out at sea chasing trawlers. How stupid when there was plenty of food on the shore.

'What did you call me?' shouted back the albatross.

'Mollymawk, sir, for that is what you are, following those trawlers all day,' the oldest brother replied.

'I can indeed see a stupid gull around these parts, but it isn't me. I haven't got myself lost chasing doughnuts.'

'How do you know we are lost?'

'I heard you squawking about it and a lot of noise you were making too.'

'What are you doing out here moll …, I mean albatross, sir?' asked a second brother.

'Why, I'm following the fishing trawlers.'

'But they only have fish!'

'Ah, this one has shrimp,' smiled the albatross. 'Shrimp are delicious.'

The brothers knew of shrimp. The humans ate them in tiny polystyrene pots. Shrimp were tasty indeed. 'Where is it, I cannot see a ship,' complained the third seagull brother.

'I can. I can fly high and fast, and I can see ships miles away. There is one over there.' The albatross pointed with his beak.

'Can you see the shore from where you are?' asked a seagull brother.

'No, but I know how to find it,' replied the wise old albatross.

'Tell us! Tell us!' said the brothers all at once, still bobbing along on the ocean currents.

'You'll have to fly with me to the trawler. The trawlers always return to shore,' replied the albatross, and started to fly away.

'Wait for us!' the gulls cried, as the dragged themselves from the sea and up into the sky, their wings glistening with water and sugar.

They had to work hard to keep up with the albatross but, sure enough, he led them straight to the shipping trawler and what's more, he had been correct about the shrimp. Delicious! They ate their fill and soon the trawler headed back to the shore. The albatross bid the brothers farewell and they thanked their new friend.

Finally, the brother gulls found themselves safe on their familiar seaside boulevard once more, although every now and then they now follow a fishing trawler too – just to see if they can find more of those fresh shrimps. I tell you what, though, the brothers never called the albatross a Mollymawk again.

Activities

Rock Pooling

Rock pooling is a great activity for all the family. There are all sorts of tiny creatures that live in the rock pools of our shores. You might even spot Herman the hermit crab!

You will need:
* bucket, clear plastic container, large plastic bottle
* Adventure Journal
* a pen or pencil
* appropriate clothing and footwear as the rocks are slippery and wet once the tide is out
* camera (optional)
* seashore guidebook or access to one online to identify your finds

What to do:
Once you've found a suitable beach with rock pools to visit, look at the weather forecast for that day and the tide times. It is preferable to choose a dry, calm day so it's easier to see beneath the surface of the rock pool's water.

It is important to know what time the tide is coming in and out for two reasons. One, you will only be able to see the rock pools when the tide is at its lowest point and two, you need to stay safe and know when the tide is coming back in, so you are not cut off from the beach.

When you've spotted a rock pool you want to investigate, try to approach it so that your shadow does not fall across it and frighten the animals in the pool.

Next, crouch or sit on the rocks around the pool and observe the rock pool and its creatures. You may need to wait a while before the animals show themselves and you will need to focus on the water past your reflection.

Look at the different layers within the rock pool: the anemones and limpets on the sides of the pool, the blennies and crabs on the bottom and the shrimp scooting around in the middle. You could try gently lifting a stone or a rock to see what's under it. You may be lucky and crab or two will come scuttling out.

You could also try dipping your bucket into the pool and seeing what you can scoop out. Try to do this as gently as possible. Using a net when rock pooling is not advisable as many of the creatures are tiny and have soft bodies, which may be damaged by the net.

In your Adventure Journal, make a note of what you have found. You could take some pictures of the creatures to stick into the book and even draw some of them if you want.

Once you have finished observing them, always release the animals back into the pool they came from and always leave the place as you found it, taking your belongings and any rubbish home with you.

What you might spot:
- beadlet anemones
- hermit crabs
- blennies
- gobies
- shells
- fossils
- barnacles
- limpets
- mussels
- dog whelks
- seaweed, such as bladderwrack
- green shore crab
- edible crab
- porcelain crab
- mermaid's purse or dogfish eggs
- starfish
- shrimp or common prawn.

Who has Legs?

There are thought to be 1 million species of animals who live in the ocean. In the story of 'How the Whale got his Barnacles', the whale goes in search of animals that have legs and live in the sea. For this activity, you too can go in search of the creatures who live in the sea. There are three ways you could do this, below.

A Trip to the Beach

On your trip out rock pooling, you could also look at what creatures are in the sea. You will have to make sure the tide has come in a bit more for this, and that you are standing somewhere safe and will not be cut off by the incoming tide. As always, ask an adult to help you and make sure you are wearing the correct clothing and footwear, as you will be paddling in the sea. You could even go bare foot and roll up your trousers legs.

To observe creatures under the water, you are going to need something called a bathyscope or aquascope. You can of course buy one of these, but you can also make one with an old plastic bottle and some cling film.

Cut the top and bottom off the bottle and stretch cling film, a plastic bag or another type of thin plastic tightly over one end of the bottle. Secure the cling film or plastic with an elastic band or strong tape.

Hold the bottle with the cling film end in the water – don't put the bottle in too deep or water will go in the bottle – and then look into the top of the bottle to see what creatures are swimming around your feet. You will need to stay still for a while before any creatures will come near. Write down what you spot in your Adventure Journal. Which creatures had legs and which didn't?

A Trip to an Aquarium

If you have a local aquarium you can visit, then why not go and see what wonders of the deep you can find there. Have a think before you go about which creatures might have legs and which don't.

When you are there, make a note in your Adventure Journal and compare it with the notes you made before your trip. Were you right? How many creatures with legs did you spot?

A Trip to your Local Fish Market or Fish Counter

If you are unable to visit the beach or an aquarium, your local fish counter or fish market will have lots of sea creatures for you to look at. Perhaps you could even buy some (preferably sustainably caught) to take home and cook in a wonderful fish stew called bouillabaisse.

You could try drawing some of them in your Adventure Journal or taking some pictures while you are there. What was the catch of the day? Did the fishmonger have creatures with legs, too, or just fins?

Sea Creature Tic-Tac-Toe

Tic-Tac-Toe, or Noughts and Crosses as it's also known, is a super simple game for two people. For this activity, you are going to see if you can help the nautilus deliver his message across the tic-tac-toe board by creating a row of three nautilus across the board, either diagonally, horizontally or vertically. But watch out, because shrimp might get there first. Below are some instructions on how to create your own tic-tac-toe board and game pieces.

For this activity you will need:

* small 3cm × 3cm picture of a nautilus (drawn, printed or photocopied)
* small 3cm × 3cm picture of a shrimp (drawn, printed or photocopied)
* old cardboard box like a cereal box
* marker pen

How to make your game:

Find a picture of a nautilus and a shrimp in a book or online. Draw or print out five copies of the nautilus and five copies of the shrimp. Each individual nautilus or shrimp should be approximately 3cm × 3cm in size.

Next, cut out a piece of card approximately 12cm × 12cm.

On the plain side of the card, use the marker pen to mark out a nine-square grid. Each square should be 4cm × 4cm.

You should now have a playing board (the grid), five separate nautili and five separate shrimp.

You are ready to play.

How to play:

Decide who is the nautilus and who is the shrimp and then decide who is going to go first. That person places one of their animals in one of the boxes on the tic-tac-toe grid.

Now it's the second player's turn to place one of their animals in one of the squares.

The game continues until one person has created a row of three of the same animals (nautilus or shrimp), vertically, horizontally or diagonally. Don't forget, you can block each other's way too, but this might end in a draw and then no one gets their message delivered!

Doughnut Style Muffins

Makes 12

Ingredients
200g plain flour
1 tbsp baking powder
½ tsp salt
50g caster sugar
50g butter
1 large egg
200ml milk
strawberry jam
50g icing sugar for dusting
¼ tsp ground cinnamon

Method
- Preheat your oven to 160°C. Take a twelve-cup muffin tin and if you are not using muffin cases, then you will need to butter the muffin tin cups.
- Measure out the milk, add the egg and beat. Melt the butter and leave to cool for a couple of minutes.
- Add the flour, baking powder, salt and caster sugar to a large bowl. Add the milk mixture and the butter and whisk until combined well.
- Add mixture to the cases until they are one-third full. Add a teaspoon of strawberry jam on top of the mixture in each case. Now, divide the remaining mixture between the cases, covering the jam.
- Place the muffins in the oven and cook for 20–25 minutes until golden and the top springs back to the touch.
- Take the muffins out of the oven and leave them to cool on a cooling rack. Meanwhile, mix the icing sugar and cinnamon together.
- Once the muffins have cooled, sift the icing sugar and cinnamon mix on the tops of the muffins. You could do this by using a sieve or tea strainer.
- And there you have it – doughnut muffins! But watch out for those seagulls.

August

Waves of wheat in the fields
The harvest is almost here
A time of plenty for all
When fruits of labour appear

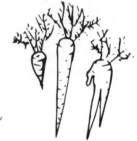

The Tale of Three Carrots

Once upon a time, in a walled garden just down the lane, there were three carrots. They had each spent two months underground growing from a seed. They were ready to greet the sunshine and talked about it excitedly.

'Why are you so keen to be picked?' asked a passing snail. 'You are only destined for a stew.'

'Oh no, not I,' said the smallest, dainty carrot. 'I am far too small and not worth eating. The gardener will surely throw me on the compost heap and then I can run away across the field.'

'Don't be silly. He'll eat you first!' said the snail.

'He won't eat me,' said the long, thin carrot. 'I am a fine example of a carrot and he will surely take me to the village show where I will win first prize. Then I can run away and be free.'

The snail scoffed. 'You're a perfect stewing carrot!'

'Well, he definitely won't eat me,' said the last carrot, who was all lumpy and misshapen. 'I'm far too knobbly and bobbly. He won't go to the bother of peeling me. I'll probably be made into a vegetable animal by his daughter and treasured for ever more.'

It was all too much for the snail and he crawled off, laughing all the way.

Sure enough, the gardener came into the garden and saw the tops of the carrots peaking up above the soil like tiny orange sunrises. 'Ooh, lovely,' he said, bending down to pick the smallest carrot. 'You will be lovely and sweet, it seems such a shame to cook you.' The gardener pondered the tiny carrot for a moment and then brushed off the soil, snapped off his green leaves and ate him in one bite. 'Delicious,' he said wiping his mouth with the back of his hand.

Next, he pulled up the long, thin carrot and then the knobbly one. 'What a pair you are,' he said. 'I have just the jobs for you.' And he walked back into the house. The two carrots winked at each other – they were sure they would not be eaten now.

Placing the knobbly carrot on the windowsill, the gardener washed the long, thin carrot and placed it on the chopping board. The third carrot watched from the windowsill as the gardener began to cut the long, thin carrot up and put it into his bubbling stew. The knobbly carrot crossed its bobbly arms and felt very smug. It was surely safe now, sitting on the windowsill.

After dinner, the gardener took the knobbly, bobbly carrot from the windowsill and walked to the end of the garden. The knobbly carrot had hoped to stay on the windowsill, but nevertheless the compost was at the bottom of the garden and perhaps that's where the gardener was heading; at least then it could escape into the fields. But the gardener walked past the compost heap and through the gate into the field. The gardener gave a whistle and an old shire horse trotted across the field towards the gardener's outstretched hand, which held the knobbly, bobbly carrot. The carrot had no time to think of what might have been before the old shire horse gobbled it up. Which just goes to show that sometimes you can't fight destiny.

A New-Found Strength

There is a little shrub in a large pot by my back door and when I sit on the threshold of the house to drink a cup of tea in the sunshine, as I often do, I sometimes hear a chattering from beneath its shiny green leaves. The other day, the chattering got ever so loud, so I peered into the shrub to see what all the commotion was about. Can you imagine my surprise when, on one of the sturdier branches, I saw three beetles arguing?

As I looked in, a bright green chafer beetle was the first to speak. 'I'm the biggest, so I am clearly the strongest,' he said. 'I could lift the pot this shrub is in right off the ground – no problem.' As he spoke, he was busy polishing the glistening shell that housed his wings. His arrogance was astounding, and I watched on, waiting to see if I would witness this amazing feat of strength.

Next, it was the stag beetle's turn to put his case forward. He was a bold, glossy black beetle with enormous antlers.

'Piffle,' he announced. 'My antlers would lift this pot in a flash, much quicker than you ever could.'

'Ha!' the earwig chipped in. 'You think you're both so big and strong but sometimes the smallest beetles have the most strength when tested!'

'Don't make us laugh,' said the chafer. 'This is a job for big beetles. I don't see how you could even suggest that you could manage to lift this pot!'

'It's a ridiculous notion,' the stag beetle agreed.

'Well, I could!' she said. 'I have a way of getting into small spaces. I could wriggle underneath to the bottom of the pot and lift it, no problem.'

Transfixed, I watched as the chafer and stag beetles rolled around the branch, laughing at the little earwig.

'I'll show you!' huffed the earwig and started to make her way to the bottom of the pot.

Now, everyone knows that you really shouldn't laugh at those who are smaller or weaker than yourself, you never know what hidden strengths they may have, so I decided to teach the chafer and stag beetles a lesson.

Once I saw the earwig was under the pot, I stood up and lifted the pot off the ground.

'Whoa!' shouted the bigger beetles, struggling to hold on to the branch. I made sure the little earwig had a chance to scuttle away before I put the pot down again and sat back down with my cup of tea.

The chaffer and the stag beetles peered over the rim of the pot and looked down at the earwig as she climbed back up. They were astounded.

'What a mighty little bug you are,' the stag beetle said. 'Come and join us – tell us more of your courage and strength, little earwig.'

And the earwig did. They spent the afternoon telling stories of bravery and the near misses they'd had in the garden. I very much enjoyed listening to them as I drank my tea and, I can tell you this, the other beetles never underestimated the little earwig ever again.

The Mouse in the Windmill

High up on a hill, across the babbling brook, there is a little windmill. It works hard all day, grinding flour for the miller who sells it to the baker. The miller is a miserly fellow who is paid well for his flour, but he does not like to part with the money he earns, so the windmill is neglected. He spends the minimum he can to get the maximum from the windmill. There are cogs that could do with extra oil, gears that could do with some grease and there are always holes in the sails that need patching. If all these things were fixed, it would mean the windmill wouldn't have to work quite as hard.

Under the stairs that lead to the top of the windmill, where the cogs are that run the sails, lives a little mouse. He spends the day looking for food. You would think that would be easy in a windmill full of corn, but the miller keeps it all locked up so tight that all the mouse gets is the odd husk and crumb of flour that falls from the millstones as they move round and round.

'I wish I was appreciated more,' sighed the windmill, one day. It was hot and the sails turned slowly in the midday sun, every movement stiff and stilted. 'I just need a little oil on my cogs and my sails would move more easily.'

'I think I can help you there,' said the mouse, seeing an opportunity.

'Oh? How?' asked the windmill.

'If you let me, I will take one of your cogs and hide it. Then the miller will have to stop milling and look for it. When he puts it back, he will surely oil your cogs.'

'Good idea!' said the windmill, who liked the idea of having a rest.

So, the mouse hurried into the workings of the windmill and worked loose a cog. He took it back to his mouse hole and hid it.

The sails of the windmill gradually ground to a halt and the miller scratched his head. 'What's happened now?' he said to himself.

Climbing the stairs, he entered the room where all the cogs and gears were and started to look through them. 'Ah,' he said, 'I see the problem, there's a cog missing.'

Getting down on his hands and knees, he searched for the cog, but he couldn't find it anywhere. Standing up, he came face to face with the little mouse, who was standing on a wooden beam.

'Hello,' said the mouse. 'Are you looking for something?'

'Shoo! Bothersome mouse, no doubt you intend to eat my wheat!' The miller reached for the broom that was propped up against the wall.

'I wouldn't do that if I were you,' said the mouse. 'I can help you.'

'You!' sneered the miller. 'How can you help me?'

'I know where that cog is,' the mouse said, pointing at the space where the cog should be.

'Did you take it?' asked the miller, frowning. 'Why, I should beat you with this broom!'

'And then you'd never find that cog!' smiled the mouse. 'Of course, I'm happy to return it but we have some conditions.'

'We?' said the miller, confused.

'Yes, we. Me and the windmill.'

'The windmill?'

'Yes!'

When the miller heard that, he laughed and laughed. 'No matter, little mouse, I will get a new cog.' And so the miller did, but that night the mouse stole it again.

This went on for many days until the mouse wondered if he'd have room for all the cogs in his mouse hole. He was very careful not to be caught and the miller got angrier and angrier. Every day the windmill's sails stayed still, and the miller could not earn money for his flour. Finally, his wife could take no more.

'We have no money for food!' she exclaimed. 'We don't even have flour for bread.'

The miller, frustrated by the little mouse, told her the story of the mouse and the cog. She laughed and laughed. 'Get a mousetrap,' she said.

And so the miller did, but the mouse wasn't silly. In the middle of the night the mouse crept up to the miller's bedroom, dragging the trap behind him and left it under the miller's big hairy toe that was hanging out of the bed sheets. As soon as the miller moved in his sleep – snap!

'Yaowww!' screeched the miller.

'What is the matter?' cried his wife, as she woke with a start. When she saw the trap on the miller's toe, she laughed and laughed.

'Buy a cat!' she said.

So, the miller bought a cat, but he didn't feed it because he didn't want to spend the money on its food and he wanted it to catch the mouse. The cat soon got annoyed that it never had anything to eat and it really didn't like mice, so when the mouse left a note in his dish one night telling him there was better food in the village, the cat ran away.

The cogs were still going missing and the windmill still wasn't working. A whole month had gone by and the village baker, with his flour reserves used up, was threatening to go elsewhere for his flour.

'That's it!' said the miller when he found the cat gone. 'I've had enough. Come out little mouse. What is it you want?'

The mouse crawled out from under kitchen table and smiled up at the miller. 'Not much, just a few ears of corn every day to feed my hungry belly and some proper maintenance for the poor windmill.'

'Fine!' said the miller, finally beaten and happy to do anything to get the windmill working again and stop his wife complaining. The mouse ran away to fetch one of the cogs.

'Remember,' the mouse said when he returned, 'if you don't hold up your side of the bargain, a little cog might go missing again.'

The mouse smiled at the miller's frown but the miller kept his end of the bargain, most of the time. If ever the miller started to let the windmill's maintenance slip or forgot to leave corn for the mouse, he was reminded with a cog sitting on the breakfast table in the morning. The windmill and the mouse were very happy and the miller, well, he would always be a grumpy old miller – but at least he could sell his flour again.

Peace Pizza

The people of Pinavia had been at war with each other for many years. In the north, the pig farmers fought for land to keep their pigs on and could not understand why the corn farmers in the east wanted to grow an extra row of sweetcorn when they already had plenty. The sweetcorn farmers complained about the smell from the pigs and the hogs that ate the corn on the edge of their fields. They also argued with the olive growers in the south and said their olive tree roots stole valuable water from their sweetcorn crops.

The olive growers complained that the towering corn blocked the sunlight from the olive groves and that the goat herders in the west allowed their herds to eat the olives off the trees. The goat herders, who made goat's cheese, complained the olives curdled the goats' milk and that the pigs in the north chased the goats.

Finally, the pig farmers complained the goats kept straying onto their land and eating the pig food. No one was happy!

In the middle of town there was a pizzeria owned by Alberto. Alberto was fed up with hearing the complaints from the different farmers when they came into the pizza shop. Even worse, if the pig farmers were in the restaurant none of the other farmers would come in and vice versa. And if that wasn't bad enough, the pig farmers would only eat ham pizzas, the olive growers would only eat olive pizzas, the sweetcorn farmers only wanted sweetcorn and the goat herders only wanted goat's cheese pizzas.

It was a lot of work for Alberto, who was an easy-going fellow and wanted a peaceful life. So, he came up with a plan.

Alberto set about making an enormous pizza – the biggest pizza that would fit in his oven. On one quarter he put ham, the second quarter had olives, another quarter had sweetcorn and on the last he put goat's cheese. He then put the pizza in the oven and sent an anonymous invitation to each of the four sets of farmers to come to Alberto's for free pizza that evening.

Sure enough, they all arrived and immediately the arguing began, but when Alberto pulled the pizza from the oven, a hush fell as the farmers took in the sight of the incredible creation.

'What is that?' asked a corn farmer.

'A peace pizza!' said Alberto, placing the pizza down on some tables he'd pushed together. Around the tables were seats and Alberto gestured to the to farmers. 'Sit! Eat!' he smiled.

'I'm not sitting with them,' said a pig farmer, drawing his eyes to slits as he looked at one of the goat herders.

'Sit next to the olive growers then,' reasoned Alberto.

A wonderful smell rose from the pizza – ham mingled with the olives and the aroma of sharp goat's cheese danced with the sweet smell of corn.

'It would be a shame to waste such a fine pizza,' said an olive grower.

'True enough,' a corn farmer echoed the sentiment.

Chairs scraped on the stone floor, the only thing to break the silence as they all sat around the pizza. With sideways glances and hunched shoulders, they began to eat.

'These olives are perfect,' said an olive grower. 'Succulent and fresh.'

'Not as fresh as this cheese,' a goatherd announced. 'Fantastically sharp and tangy.'

'This ham is surely worth the effort,' said a pig farmer. 'A savoury delight.'

'Not as delightful as this juicy sweetcorn,' said a corn farmer.

Soon the room was once more filled with arguing voices. Cutting across them all, Alberto shouted, 'Why don't you all try each other's pizza?'

The farmers stopped talking and looked at each other, shocked by the suggestion. A pig farmer was the first to try a slice of the olive pizza. 'This goes so well with the ham,' he said.

The olive grower took a slice of the goat's cheese pizza. 'This tangy cheese really compliments my fresh olives!'

The corn grower took a slice of the ham pizza next. 'The perfect mix of sweet and savoury,' she said.

The room filled with voices again, only this time they were swapping pizza slices, complimenting each other and even mixing the ingredients together.

Now, every year, the villagers gather at Alberto's for an enormous pizza and they each contribute ingredients from their farms. The pizza no longer has separate quarters and the ham, sweetcorn, olives and goat's cheese are all mixed together in a harmony of flavours that now reflects the peace that reigns between the farmers of Pinavia. All thanks to Alberto!

Activities

Visit a Pick-Your-Own Farm

The gardener in 'The Tale of Three Carrots' could not resist those tasty vegetables. Growing your own food is a great way to learn about vegetables, but another way to gather your own food is to visit a pick-your-own farm. There are many places you can do this across the country.

Picking your own food is a great way to connect with the earth and the produce it gives us. As you are picking different fruit and vegetables, have a little look to see which ones grow on bushes, which grow in the ground, which ones grow on trees and which grow on vines. Why not take your Adventure Journal and draw a sketch of the fruit on the plant and make notes about how it's growing?

Each farm will grow different things, so if you want to pick a particular fruit or vegetable, remember to check the farm you are going to grows it. Perhaps you could see if you can find some ingredients for your very own Peace Pizza, featured in this set of activities.

Here are some of the fruit and vegetables you might find at pick-your-own farms at this time of year:

* broccoli
* carrots
* peas
* spinach
* runner beans
* sweetcorn
* squash
* strawberries
* blackcurrants
* redcurrants
* raspberries
* blueberries
* blackberries
* plums.

Bug Hunt

The bugs I found under my garden pot are only a few of the insects you may find in your back garden. There are 27,000 different types of insects in the UK alone. For this activity, we are going to see how many we can find in a 50cm square patch of our garden. If you don't have a garden, you could visit your local green space or a public garden for this activity.

What you will need:
* 2 metres of string
* tape measure
* bug viewer or empty, clean see-through container
* magnifying glass (optional)
* Adventure Journal
* pen
* insect ID guide (there is a link in the back of the book to an online guide).

Method:
Find a suitable patch of ground (for example, on grass or in the soil) and lay your string out in a square shape, with each side measuring 50cm. Once you have your square, you can start to have a look at what animals you can find inside it.

If you are able, you could try gently placing an insect in a bug viewer or an empty tub to get a closer look. If you have a magnifying glass, you'll be able to get an even closer look. Make a note of them in your Adventure Journal and try drawing them if you can. Always put the bugs back where you found them.

Some beetles in this country, like the stag beetle, are extremely rare and classified as endangered, so if you do see one, try not to disturb them.

Once you've looked at all the bugs in one square, you could try a different habitat and move your square to a tree, hanging the string from the branches, or take a look at the flowers in a border. If the border is in a park or wildflower meadow, try not to step into the border or damage the plants as you are looking for your bugs.

What bugs you might find:
* ants
* bumblebees
* heath bee-flies

* spiders
* crickets
* grasshoppers
* ladybirds
* daddy longlegs
* shield bugs
* earwigs
* butterflies
* black clock beetle
* broad ground beetle
* cardinal beetle.

Pause as the Wheel Turns

Lammas

Lammas is the first of the harvest festivals in the wheel of the year. It's a celebration of the golden crenulations of wheat that stand tall in the fields, ready to be harvested. Celebrated on 1 or 2 August, Lammas marks the end of the summer season as the tell-tale signs of autumn start to appear. Sunsets are a little earlier, the fruit is swelling in the trees and the flowers begin to wilt and drop their seeds.

This may seem early for a harvest festival, but with advances in modern technology, the time and way grain is harvested has now changed, whereas in a slower time, when machines were not available, the crops would have been harvested in one go.

Traditionally bread is the way to celebrate Lammas, so why not have a go at baking your own? Listen to the thud and phut of the dough and get stuck in.

Corn dollies are also a great way to celebrate. Plait in your hopes and dreams, what you wish to harvest this autumn, and give thanks to the earth that grew the corn, the fire of the sun that warmed it, the water that fed it and the wind that carried the seed.

However you celebrate, be sure to enjoy the last of the long summer evenings, perhaps with a tall glass of barley water.

Make a Windmill

If you are lucky, there may be a windmill near you that you could visit and, if it's a working windmill, see how the miller makes the grain into flour. For this activity, you can make your own simple mini-windmill. It won't grind grain into flour, but you might be able to get the sails to turn if there's enough wind.

What you will need:
* large, clean empty yogurt pot (the 400g kind)
* coloured pens/paint
* two large lollipop sticks
* bradawl or screwdriver (for your adult to use)
* a split-pin paper fastener.

How to make your windmill:
Turn your yogurt pot upside down so the opening is at the bottom. Decorate your yogurt pot with windows and a door. This is the main body of your windmill and you can design it however you would like.

Next, ask an adult to make a hole in the middle of both lollipop sticks, equal distances from both ends. Your adult will need a sharp bradawl for this job, or a screwdriver. The hole needs to be big enough to fit the split pin through.

Next, get your adult to make a hole about 3cm from the top of your upside-down yogurt pot. Place the lollipop sticks in a cross shape and thread the split pin through the two sticks and then through the hole in the yogurt pot. (If your lollipop sticks catch on the ground as they turn, ask your adult to cut them down so that they can turn without catching.)

Fold back the split pins and check the lollipop sticks can move like a windmill's sail. If they don't, loosen the split pin a little until they do.

Place your windmill somewhere sunny and where the wind can catch the sails, but remember to look after it or a little mouse might move in and cause mischief.

Peace Pizza

Makes 2

Ingredients
pack of two large ready-made pizza bases
120ml passata
2 slices of ham
80g olives
2 tbsp sweetcorn
50g goat's cheese
125g grated or fresh mozzarella cheese
fresh basil leaves

Method
❉ Preheat your oven to 180°C. Place the two pizza bases on baking trays.
❉ Divide the passata between the two bases and spread evenly across each one. Split the mozzarella between the two pizzas. Sprinkle evenly over the base if using grated mozzarella or slice if using fresh mozzarella. On one quarter of each pizza place the ham, on the second quarter add the olives, sliced if preferred, on the third quarter place the sweetcorn and to the last quarter add goat's cheese. (These ingredients can be changed as long as there are four different ingredients, one on each quarter of the pizza.)
❉ Now scatter fresh basil leaves to your taste over the pizzas and place the pizzas in the oven for 10 minutes.

September

Here it is, the autumn, and the trees all bear their fruit
Beneath, the animals gather supplies and hide it under roots
Spiders seek the warmth inside to build their webs and beds
This is the time of plenty before the winter's test.

Time for a Rest

A grandfather clock stood in the corner of the squirrels' treetop house and waited. Tick-tock, tick-tock. He waited … waited for the squirrels to stand still, take time to talk to each other and rest. But the squirrels never did.

If they weren't collecting nuts for dinner, they were rushing around arranging important meetings of the High Squirrels, organising nut collections and winter storage for the community. They were hard-working squirrels, the clock observed, but they never seemed to talk about anything else except work.

So, the clock had an idea. He stopped working. On purpose. No accident. And he stopped around teatime.

The squirrel family who lived in his tree had all returned for a meal of hazelnut soup and acorn bread before commencing their toils once more. The squirrels had a strict regime. Five o' clock to five fifteen, that was how long they allowed themselves to eat.

Finishing his soup, the biggest squirrel looked up from his dinner. 'I ate that quick!' he said, noting the clock read five minutes past five.

'So did I,' said the other big squirrel.

'And me,' said the smallest.

Sitting back in their chairs, they began to talk. They talked about the nut collection and how many more nuts they had to gather before winter. The hands of the clock did not move.

Soon they ran out of things to say about work, and they started to talk of other things. How the beech trees were particularly beautiful this year, what a warm September they were having. And then they started to talk about little squirrel's day. How she had collected fireflies in a jar at school for her room, and how she would love to go down to the stream and paddle in the water before she went to bed.

'We have time,' said the biggest squirrel, smiling and seeing that the clock had not moved on.

And so they all walked down to the stream. They listened to the different birds that were singing, watched the butterflies dancing through the meadow and finally bathed their hot, busy feet in the cool, running stream. They played there until the sun began to set and the fish swam away to hide in the reeds. By the time they got home to their tree, the sun had almost set.

'It's late,' said the big squirrel. 'We haven't collected any nuts and now we're behind.'

'Sorry,' said the little squirrel.

'What for?' said the other big squirrel.

'I was having fun,' said the little squirrel.

'We all were,' said the other big squirrel. 'There is no need for sorry. We'll collect the nuts we need tomorrow. Rest is important too. Even the clock was having a rest!' she noted, as she saw the clock still said five minutes past five.

When the clock heard this, he smiled. At last, they had seen what he had seen. Spending time playing was just as important as working and he began to tick again. Tick-tock, tick-tock.

The Three Brother Magpies

Magpies are very good at storing food. When there is plenty of food around for them to eat, they start to hide it in the ground ready for the winter months, just like squirrels do, and this is the story of three brother magpies who do just that.

Just over the hill, across the meadow, over the stile and into a golden field of corn there stands a tall oak tree. It has been there for almost a hundred years and has seen many things. In the tree live three brother magpies. They live a life of plenty and never want for food, even in the harsh winter months. Their secret is that they all have a job. Each knows his role and does it well.

The first magpie can sing. Now, when I say sing, I mean he whispers to the clouds, entreats the sun and lulls the grass to sleep at night. He is a charmer – in particular, a beetle charmer. When the beetles hear him sing, they push their heads out of their hiding places to listen.

The second magpie is as fast as lightning. His beak is needle sharp and his light-footed hopping is barely audible to the poor beetles, who are snapped up as soon as the first magpie begins to sing. The second magpie catches so many beetles that they can easily afford to store them for winter, deep in the ground beneath the old oak tree.

The third magpie is strong, and he digs the hole beneath the tree to put the beetles in. He catches the beetles as his middle brother throws them to him and tucks them safely into one of the holes he has dug. In this way, the three brothers work in harmony together, gathering beetles for the winter and they live a happy life.

One day, the second magpie had a thought. 'Wouldn't it be nice,' he said to his brothers, 'if I could do the singing for a bit. I am tired of having to concentrate so hard on catching the beetles. My eyes could do with a rest.'

'My beak could certainly do with some respite,' said the third magpie. 'I am tired of having a beak full of mud all the time. How about you dig some holes instead of singing?' he said to the first magpie.

'Easy,' said the first magpie. He believed the only true talent between the three of them was his singing and thought digging a hole could hardly be difficult.

The next day the magpies awoke, all ready for a new day with new jobs. The third magpie waited on the ground for the second magpie to start singing and the first magpie leant against the tree and waited.

The second magpie cleared his throat and began to sing. It was such a cacophony that the rooks in the nearby wood started to laugh. The beetles came out from their hiding places, but only to see what the awful noise was.

The third magpie, muscular and strong, was not as agile as the second and could not move as fast, nor was he as light footed. He caught only three beetles in the time it would normally take his brother to catch ten.

The first magpie began his task, thinking he would easily dig a hole, but as he started his beak filled with mud and it became harder and harder to dig. He had only dug half a hole in the time it took his brother to dig two.

Finally, the second magpie's throat became sore from singing. 'I must get a drink,' he said. 'Why don't you start putting the beetles you've caught into the ground and I will be back in a bit.'

The first magpie tried to fit the beetles they had caught in the hole but the store he had dug simply wasn't big enough. 'It's no use,' he huffed. 'I think this soil must be tougher than usual.'

'I'll do it,' said the third magpie, not wishing his beetle-catching efforts to have been in vain, and he started to dig in the ground with ease. Finally, the second magpie returned after quenching his thirst and the three perched on a branch of the oak tree staring solemnly at the sun as it reached its midday height.

'We'll never catch enough beetles to see us through winter at this rate,' sighed the first magpie.

'We should go back to what we are good at,' said the third magpie.

'Agreed,' said the second.

And so they did.

An observer would think it was the wind that rustled the old oak tree's leaves, but no, the tree was actually laughing gently at the silly birds.

From Little Acorns

There once was a chestnut tree that lived next door to an oak tree. Of all the trees in the wood, they were the tallest. Of course, they were always competing with each other.

The oak tree held onto the last of his leaves to try and prove it was the strongest. The last shrivelled oak leaf would always fall a second after those of the chestnut tree. The chestnut tree grew the most fragrant flowers it possibly could, tall spires of pink and white blooms that attracted many more bees than the oak could ever hope to.

The one thing they could not decide on, though, was whose fruit was the best.

'The squirrels love my acorns,' said the oak, one day. 'They can't get enough of them for their winter stores!'

'The children love my conkers,' boasted the chestnut tree. 'Their smiles are worth a million of your acorns.'

'Ah, but which of your fruit is the tastiest?' shouted a jay from a birch tree nearby.

'Mine!' shouted the oak and the chestnut trees together.

'Why don't I judge that?' said the jay, with a smile. 'Why don't you each shake me a nice pile of chestnuts or acorns to eat and I'll let you know.'

Now, what the chestnut and oak trees didn't know was that the jay was lazy, and he did like acorns, but he loved chestnuts more. He knew that the chestnut tree would want to win so badly that it would pile up the chestnuts for him. He would be able to gorge himself on them. And that's exactly what he did.

When he had finished the chestnuts, he wiped his beak in the grass and looked at the pile of acorns. 'I'm too full to eat the acorns,' he said with a burp. 'I declare the chestnut the winner.'

'But that wasn't fair!' shouted the oak tree. But the jay was long gone; off to his tree to sleep off the many chestnuts he had eaten.

The pile of acorns stayed where it was, a painful reminder to the oak tree never again to trust a jay. The chestnut tree goaded him with its victory.

The jay had such a stomach ache from eating all the chestnuts that he never ate chestnuts again and that's why jays prefer acorns. However, our story doesn't end there.

Next year, where the pile of acorns lay, new shoots appeared. Years passed and years more and, in time, a little acorn forest grew. Eventually, many oaks surrounded the chestnut tree. There were no more chestnut trees growing as the conkers had not been allowed to bury themselves in the ground. They had all been eaten by the jay or collected by children instead.

The chestnut tree could not argue with the might of all those oak trees, as they grew taller and taller, around it. The moral of this story? Not all victories are what they seem.

Always in a Hurry

As you know, millipedes are always in a rush. How could they not be when they have hundreds of legs? Now, this particular millipede was hurrying home one day after a hard day's foraging. She didn't have much to offer her family for dinner. In her basket were a few leaves of wild garlic and some tiny white sorrel flowers; it was enough if they mixed it with some of the grain they had in their store. But she was late, and her husband would be waiting for the ingredients to cook for the family and the little millipedes would be hungry.

As she was scurrying home across the earth, twigs and dry leaves, she heard a cry for help. Now, this millipede had a good heart and despite being in a terrible rush, she left her path home to find out who needed help. As she rounded a blade of grass, she saw a ladybird.

'My house is on fire!' cried the ladybird.

'Don't worry,' said the millipede. 'Give me all the buckets, bowls and jugs you have. I can carry them on my many legs and I will bring water back for you to put out the fire.'

The ladybird did as she was asked and the millipede went to a nearby pool of water, filled the many vessels and scampered back. The fire was extinguished and the house saved. The ladybird was so grateful that she gave the millipede her last jar of honey. The millipede tried to refuse but the ladybird insisted, and the millipede placed the jar in her basket and carried on home.

She hadn't been walking for long when she heard someone crying – a tiny, choked sob. The sun was starting to dip in the sky and she knew she really should be getting home, but the millipede had to find out who was upset. Following the sound to the bottom of the old oak tree, she saw a tiny caterpillar.

'I can't reach the branch up there. It would be just wonderful for my cocoon.'

'Don't worry,' said the millipede. 'I will stand on my hind legs and you can climb up me to reach the branch.'

The caterpillar dried his eyes and thanked the millipede many times. When he was safely on his branch, he was so happy to be in the perfect spot that he threw down some of the tree's acorns for the millipede.

'You can make flour with these,' he shouted. The millipede thanked him, added them to her basket and ran on along the path.

It was getting late now, and she knew her family would be wondering where she was. It was then she heard an angry voice: 'Bother!'

On the horizon, the sun was tinged with pink and had almost reached the tops of the grass in the meadow, but the millipede could not walk by if another animal needed her. Lifting a piece of bark, she saw what the problem was. A little dung beetle was standing next to his cart, hands on hips, frowning. One of the wheels had come off.

'Don't worry,' smiled the millipede. 'I will roll my body up tight and you can use me as a wheel to get home.' And so she did.

Well, the dung beetle couldn't believe his luck. He felt sure he would never have got home without her help and now the millipede had strayed far from her original path. He looked around his little house for something to give her by way of thanks.

'Here, have these blackberries. They are freshly picked today.'

The millipede started to wave them away but the dung beetle insisted she must have the blackberries and so she added them to her basket.

By now the sun had almost disappeared in the grey twilight. The millipede rushed home and as she burst through the door of their little house, she apologised a thousand times for her lateness, what little food she had in her basket, and how she had met all these people on her way home who badly needed her help. When she had finished, her husband looked down at the basket.

'What do you mean you have no food for our supper? Look at these riches you have brought us: honey, acorns to make flour and blackberries. They will make a fine crumble.'

The little millipedes' tummies rumbled and they licked their lips at the thought of blackberry crumble, and the mother millipede flopped down in a chair laughing. Helping all those other animals get home for their dinner meant that she and her family now had the most wonderful feast. She was happy as she watched her husband begin the cooking and the little millipedes gather around waiting for their delicious meal.

Activities

Geocaching

The hobby of geocaching first started in the millennial year 2000 when location satellites, initially only used by the military, became available for all. Now anyone could pinpoint a location using this global positioning system (GPS). As a result, people started to hide treasure or caches in various places around the country and then register these sites online. A little like the squirrels caching food in our story 'Time for a Rest', these caches often contain all sorts of treasure.

For this activity, we are going on a treasure hunt to find some of these geocaches.

Before you go out, you are going to need to identify which geocaches are in your area and what their co-ordinates are. You can do this by using the official website listed at the back of this book in the section called Resources.

You could use a map to try and find the caches. However, you will find them more easily if you use a GPS app on your phone and there are many of those available. The main geocaching website also has an application for your phone that you can download if you would like.

Now you've identified your caches, here's what you will need to take with you:

* appropriate clothing and footwear
* a map, a GPS, or a mobile phone with a geocaching app
* a pen to sign the logbook in the cache when you find it
* a small torch in case the caches are hidden under roots and rocks
* swag! (Many geocaches have small toys, keyrings, cards or souvenirs in them and the idea is you can swap these with your own additions to the cache. This is an entirely optional part of geocaching, though, and it will depend on the size of the cache as to what is in it. Some are micro-caches and will only contain a very small log. It's important to remember to never put anything edible in a cache and never eat anything someone has left in a cache.)

Now you're ready to go!

When you are looking for caches make sure you keep your eyes peeled. They could be under things, in things, behind things, under tree roots, hedges and benches. Some micro-caches are disguised as snails or the bolts on benches, but it's probably best to start with the regular caches first.

The website in the back of this book will tell you who placed the cache, how hard it is to find the cache, and what sort of cache it is. Once you've found it, you can log your find on the same website and join a worldwide community of geocachers. Once you get good at it, you might even want to try making your own cache!

As always, make sure you follow the Countryside Code, leave the country as you find it and take your litter home with you. Geocaching is a great way to get to know your local area, get out and breathe in some fresh air and it will certainly keep you as busy as a squirrel.

Conker Draughts Set

Towards the end of September conkers begin to fall from the trees. These are the seeds of the spiky horse chestnuts. They are easy to tell apart from their sweet chestnut cousins as the sweet chestnut is much fluffier in appearance – but don't let that fool you, they are both very spiky.

Sweet chestnuts are great to eat when cooked but horse chestnuts are not. However, you can play some great games with them and for this activity you can make a draughts set with conkers.

You will need to collect twenty-four conkers. Once you've got them home, make sure they are clean and dry and then on twelve of them put a dab of coloured paint or a small, coloured sticker. You should now have twelve plain conkers and twelve with a dab of paint or a sticker on them.

Next, you need to make your board. Take a clean piece of plain cardboard that is 24cm × 24cm from the recycling. Create a grid on the card that is made up of sixty-four squares all measuring 3cm × 3cm.

Take a black pen and colour every other square in to create a grid like the one in Figure 1 at the back of the book.

Now you're ready to play draughts.

How to play:

The player with the plain chestnuts places all twelve on the board on the black squares so that there are three rows of them. The player with the coloured chestnuts then does the same at the opposite end of the board, still on the black squares.

The aim is to capture the other player's pieces and stop them from capturing yours. You do this by moving diagonally across the board, one square at a time, towards your opponent.

If your opponent's piece is diagonally next to you and the square the other side is free, you can hop over the piece and take it. The piece you have jumped over is removed from the board.

You can take more than one piece per go, but you cannot take two in a row, there needs to be a place to land your piece in between each piece you take.

If a player's conker reaches the opposite end of the board it becomes a King and can now be moved diagonally backwards. You will need to mark this piece in some way so that you can tell, perhaps with a piece of blue tac or a sticker.

The winner is the person who manages to capture all their opponent's pieces.

Magpie Acrostic Poem

An acrostic poem is a poem that spells out a word with the first letter of each line in the poem. There are many examples of these poems and they are perfect prompts for nature writing. For this activity, all you will need is your Adventure Journal and a pen.

The three brother magpies in our second story told us of three very different personalities, and different birds certainly have different characteristics and features. Taking the name magpie, write the letters M A G P I and E horizontally in your Adventure Journal. Now think of the magpie's characteristics and see if you can start each line of your poem with a word that relates to the magpie. For example, your first two lines might be:

Mischievous tree hopping cackler
Among the branches of the old oak tree

Continue on with your poem, finding ways to describe the magpie. It doesn't have to rhyme, just concentrate on the words and finding new ways to characterise the magpie. Once you have finished, perhaps you can draw a magpie in your book and decorate your poem page with oak leaves and beetles from the story.

If you enjoy this activity, why not try creating poems with the names of other animals, plants and trees. The possibilities are endless.

Pause as the Wheel Turns

Mabon

September heralds the beginning of autumn and the autumnal equinox on the 21st. This has been known as Mabon since the 1970s. It is the time when the night and day meet in equilibrium for the third of the year's solar festivals. The daylight hours mirror the night and the earth is in balance.

The trees dip the tips of their leaves in autumn with tiny flecks of red and gold and the animals make the most of the last glut of food, gathering and storing seeds and berries for the winter. It is a time for us, too, to gather the last of our crops and preserve them for the leaner months by making pickles, jams, salted meats and freezing fruit and vegetables.

If you're gathering in the harvest this month, don't forget to make a corn dolly with the last of the wheat crops before they are stored away. The corn dolly gives the goddess of the harvest somewhere to rest, ready for next year. Even if you're not a farmer with crops to reap, there is a glut of berries in hedgerows. If you're out and about with your foraging basket, don't forget to ask the spirits of the hedgerow before you pick the fruit and only pick fruit you are sure is edible.

Blackberry and Apple Crumble

Serves 6

For this recipe, why not go out foraging to collect the blackberries or even to your local pick your own. Don't forget, though – don't eat it if you're not 100 per cent sure it's a blackberry!

Ingredients
3 dessert apples
150g blackberries
2 tbsp honey
3 tsbp water
110g butter
110g light brown sugar
160g flour
20g oats

Method

* Preheat the oven to 180°C. Grease a medium-sized oven dish. Peel, core and slice the apples and layer them in the oven dish. Wash the blackberries and add them to the dish. Sprinkle over the water and the honey and put to one side.

* In a large mixing bowl, add the flour, oats and sugar. Rub the butter into the flour mixture until you have a fine breadcrumb texture.

* Spread the flour mixture across the top of the apple and blackberries in an even layer.

* Cook on a baking tray in the oven for 25–30 minutes until the topping is golden brown and the filling is bubbling at the edges.

* Serve on its own or with cream, custard or ice cream.

October

Come with me to the Halloween Fair
Where Jack O' Lanterns hang, you'll find me there
We'll trick or treat and dress as bats
And tell our ancestor's tales of the neighbour's black cat

The Bats of the Barn

Follow me along the river, across the fields and to a farm where there are cows. Lots of cows – brown ones, black ones, spotty ones and beige ones. They swish their tales in the last of the autumn sun, enjoying the grass in the fields before the cold months roll in and they must spend more time in the barns.

That summer on the farm had been a good summer for all and the colony of bats who lived in the big barn's rafters had had many new arrivals. One of these arrivals was Bertie, a little pipistrelle. With tiny, pointy ears and a little snout, Bertie was the smallest pipistrelle in the barn and pipistrelle bats are small. They are about 5cm long and like to come out at night, so if one flew past you on a very dark night, you might miss it!

Don't worry, though, Bertie would know you were there. In fact, I doubt Bertie would come out of the barn at all because Bertie is a very timid bat. His mother, father, brothers, sisters, aunts, uncles, cousins and grandparents all live in the barn with Bertie and they aren't timid at all. In fact, every night they go out on the most amazing adventures to catch flies and moths.

Did you know that bats can catch up to 3,000 insects a night? They sure can, and these bats definitely could, except for Bertie. He was too scared to come out of the barn. He could hear the cattle huffing and scuffing, mooing and lowing in the fields at night, and he did not like the sound of those great big animals at all.

His parents would try to encourage him by telling him the cows were friendly and he'd soon see that when they came back into the barn for the winter, but Bertie really wasn't sure about that at all. In fact, the idea of having the cows in the barn just made him even more frightened and he'd wrap his wings tight around him and hide his little face.

The problem was, winter was coming and bats hibernate in the winter. They like to have a long nap when it's cold, but this means that they need to eat even more insects so that they can last through their sleep without waking up hungry. Bertie wasn't doing this, as he wouldn't come out of the barn and his parents had stopped bringing him food. He was getting hungry, but his parents needed to eat as many insects as they could ready for winter so they couldn't bring them for Bertie as well. It was time for Bertie to start finding his own food.

One very dark night when the moon was new, Bertie woke up to a horrendous racket. Loud mooing and the stamping of hooved feet echoed throughout the barn. The cows had come in for the night. Bertie didn't have time to think. He shot out of the barn door as fast as he could. He didn't want to be anywhere near those nasty, smelly beasts.

Now Bertie was outside with all the other bats, ducking and diving, swooping and sweeping around the night sky hoovering up the insects. His parents saw him and they cheered. 'Bertie! Huzzah! Bertie is out of the barn!'

All the other bats joined in now, but Bertie wasn't happy. He hung from an old apple tree and watched the other bats. He was there for a long time before his hungry belly grumbled and he finally plucked up the courage to snap up a moth that flew a bit too close to where he was hanging. It was a big, juicy moth and it tasted good. Bertie waited for another and another until, finally, he was flying around with the other bats and filling his hungry tummy with hundreds and hundreds of insects.

The sun started to rise and a hazy yellow glow spread out across the farm. The other bats returned to roost in the barn but there was no way that Bertie was going in there. Those horrible old cows were in there.

'Come back in!' said Bertie's mother. 'The sun is no good for a bat. Come and sleep in the barn.'

But Bertie shook his head and flapped his wings, 'I'm not going back in there with those dirty old smelly, noisy cows!' he shouted.

'I beg your pardon,' said a beige Jersey cow with a soft black nose and pretty black eyes. 'I am neither smelly nor dirty and I'm not making half us much noise as you are with all that screeching,' she said.

'I … I'm sorry', said Bertie, 'I didn't mean to be rude, but you are all very loud! And you do smell a bit, well, different.'

'Different maybe, but think about us having to live underneath you lot. You just let your poop fall from the sky onto us. We're just minding our own business trying to get warm and your business falls on us!'

'I never thought of that,' said Bertie. He started to feel a little bit silly that he had been so scared and moved a little closer. He hung upside down from the barn door and continued to talk to the cow. 'That must be very unpleasant.'

'It is, why do you think we make all that noise!'

Bertie had quite forgotten all his fears and a plan started to form in his head. 'How about we roost at one end of the barn and promise to just poop in one place, would that help?'

'That would be most excellent,' said the cow. 'Then we won't have to complain and it won't be so noisy!'

'Exactly', said Bertie, and he flew off to speak to the other bats.

A deal was struck and now the bats of the barn live very happily through the winter in the company of the lowing cows. The cows are warm and so are the bats, and Bertie is no longer afraid of the cows. In fact, he doesn't think they are horrible, old, smelly beasts anymore and he enjoys a bedtime story every now and then from his friend, the Jersey cow, as she tells him of her summer adventures in the fields far away from the bats of the barn.

If, At First, You Don't Succeed

There once was a spider who spent many hours each day spinning a perfect web of sparkling gossamer, only to have it knocked down every time. First, he spun a web at the bottom of the water butt. It was quiet, dark and in the cool shade away from the sun. No sooner had he spun his web than a little mouse hurried by on her way home to her nest and burst through the beautiful skeins of invisible thread.

'I'm so sorry,' she squeaked, when she realised what she had done. 'I always take this way home, I didn't realise you'd made your web here. Can I help you put it back?'

The little spider sighed. 'Don't worry', he said, 'I'll try again.'

The next day, the spider looked around and he settled on a nearby woodpile, lovely and damp and smelling of beech and pine. The sun arced across the sky and the spider knitted and knotted a web that glistened in the twilight.

Snuffle, snuffle. 'What's that?' thought the spider. 'It sounded very close.'

Then he saw a shiny, black, round nose appearing from under the woodpile. Before he could say anything, a sleepy hedgehog had pushed his way through the web and into the evening air.

'Oh no, what's this?' exclaimed the hedgehog rubbing sleep from his eyes. 'It's sticking my spines together.'

'It was my web,' said the spider, his voice very small.

'I'm sorry,' replied the hedgehog, 'but this is the entrance to my sleeping quarters. I didn't realise you'd placed your web here. How about over there?' The hedgehog pointed to the very edge of the wood pile, a place far away from the musty centre of the stack that spider had selected. It wouldn't do.

Spider sighed. 'Don't worry,' he said. 'I'll try again.'

'I need to get up higher,' thought the spider. 'All these animals on the ground are going to wreck my web. I'll climb up the fence and make the perfect hammock in that ivy bush.' And so the spider found an arrangement of ivy and twigs to string his home from, but little did he know that the ivy bush was home to the wood pigeon, who returned, right at that moment, with a beak full of worms for his chicks.

'Coo, what's that?' he said, brushing sticky threads from his wings.

'That was my home,' said the little spider with a small sob.

'So sorry,' replied the wood pigeon. 'That's right in front of my nest and I have to get to my little ones to feed them.'

'Don't worry,' sighed the spider. 'I'll try again.'

Well, the spider was fast running out of ideas. The water butt was too low, the woodpile was hedgehog's home and the ivy bush was pigeon's. Where was he going to put his web?

A door creaked open as the lady who lived in the house belonging to the garden came out to pick some flowers. The house would be warm and safe, thought the spider, and the lady had left the door open.

The spider crept in and chose a place up high near the ceiling in the corner of the room. He spent all night constructing his little palace. It had silvery turrets, strings of tiny lights that you or I could not see and a perfectly soft bed right in the middle.

The next day, when the lady was dusting her house, she looked up at the spider's web and saw it was a new, freshly spun castle for a little spider. She let it be because she knew that for as long as it was there, she would have no flies in her house. Flies are a spider's favourite meal. She was more than happy to share her space with the little spider and finally spider had found the best place to put his home.

The Cave in the Cove

There is a cave in a cove several days north of here that holds many secrets. As you walk into the cave and move deeper and deeper into the dark, dank, salty air, look back and watch as the walls at entrance of the cave cross over and create a witch's hole, through which you can see the future.

Annabella knows of this cave's secrets and visits it to escape the routine of farming life. She does not wish to learn the vital skills her father wants to teach her. Instead, she longs to hear the icy waves of the North Sea as they crash upon the shore and listen to the seabirds as they tell her of their travels across the waves to far and distant lands.

Her mother and father tolerate her love of the sea, despite talk in the village that Annabella is wayward and undisciplined. They know there will come a time when Annabella must learn how to work the land.

Taking a hunk of bread and cheese, each afternoon Annabella walks to the cave and heads to the centre of it, where there is peace in the heart of its dark walls. Through the witch's hole created by the entrance walls, she watches the sea move in and out. When the sun begins to set, she knows it is time to return home and does so reluctantly.

Over dinner, she tells her family of the things she has seen through the doorway of the cave – tales of giant longboats arriving on the shore; the confusing vision of iron warships like nothing her village could build; or great fishing trawlers she has never seen the like of, which fish the sea until there is nothing left. Her parents listen to her quietly, indulging her imagination for as long as they eat.

One day, Annabella returns early from her time in the cave. She has seen something that upset her greatly. 'There will be no ice in the sea, Papa,' she said as she arrived home.

Her father was tilling the fields and was not listening.

'There will be no crops, Papa. The sea will rise and the land will be under water.'

Her father stopped. 'Don't talk nonsense, Annabella. As long as we give thanks for the crops each year and give offerings to the gods of the north, then we shall be well provided for.'

'It won't help, Papa!'

'Silence!' Her father shouted this time. 'I will not hear you speak out against the gods. You will learn our ways and you will work the land, as I have, and my father did. I will hear no more talk of the sea and you will not return to that cave ever again.'

From that day on, Annabella was never allowed to visit the cave. Her father kept her busy on the farm and her mother taught her how to bake and provide for the family she would one day have. What they did not know was that Annabella had seen the future.

Not the next day's future, or the next, but a future that would be her children's, children's, children's. A future where the Earth's resources have been pushed to their limits, where the sun burns too bright and the world is too warm. A future where the sea will at last reclaim the land.

The Happy Pumpkin

It was 31 October: Halloween, or as some say, the Samhain – a magical time. In a field not too far from here, a little pumpkin waited patiently in her patch. She had been waiting all month for someone to come and pick her, take her home and carve spooky characters into her. It was a pumpkin's destiny and every pumpkin knew it.

'I'm going to be the scariest face on the windowsill this year,' a very large, portly pumpkin had boasted before he was picked.

'A terrible toothy grin for me,' cackled the next pumpkin to go.

'I'd love to be the scariest face on the windowsill,' thought the little pumpkin as she watched her brothers and sisters get picked. She listened to the running feet of the children as they ran through the fields and watched their grinning, excited faces.

'An unkindness of ravens will be carved on me!' one of her sisters had squealed.

'A soaring bat will be the art my owner chooses!' another shouted.

Each pumpkin couldn't wait to fulfil his or her destiny and the little pumpkin couldn't wait either. Eventually, she was the last pumpkin on the patch, and she feared she would never be picked, left for the crows to pick at and rot back into the earth, never to fulfil her true purpose. She'd spent almost six months preparing and growing for her role on someone's windowsill.

As the farmer, who owned the field, closed the gate and the sun dipped low in the sky, he walked back to where the little pumpkin lay and bent down to pick her. 'You can come home with me,' he smiled. The little pumpkin was the perfect size for his granddaughter.

She was waiting in the kitchen when the farmer arrived home. Just back from school, she was finishing off her homework and jumped up when she saw her grandfather coming in with the pumpkin. 'It's perfect, granddad, thank you!'

'What are you going to carve on it?' her granddad asked.

'The biggest smile I can. There are too many scary pumpkins around and I want this pumpkin to be the happiest pumpkin in the whole village.'

The farmer laughed and ruffled her hair. 'An excellent idea,' he said.

And when the girl had finished her carving, the little pumpkin was indeed the happiest pumpkin in the village.

Activities

Bat Watching

In October, just like the bats of the barn, the bats of the UK are looking for food to increase their fat reserves ready for their winter hibernation. For this activity, we are going to see if we can spot some bats when they are out and about on their nightly forage.

There are around eighteen species of bat found in the UK, some of them are extremely rare and therefore protected species. Bats are nocturnal mammals, so they are most active at night. If you'd like to know a little more about bats and look at some pictures of them, you can find some links to websites in the extra resources section of the book.

Below are six bats you are most likely to see on a bat watch and all of them are small enough to fit in the palm of your hand, although, because some of these species are endangered, handling a bat is not recommended unless you have a licence and know what you are doing:

* brown long-eared bat
* common pipistrelle
* Daubenton's bat
* noctule bat
* serotine bat
* soprano pipistrelle bat.

So, how do you go about bat watching? There are two ways you can do this. You could find a locally organised bat watch or walk, or have a go at seeing what you can spot in your own garden or community green space. There are often a lot more to spot than you might think.

If you are going to have a go yourself, first you will want to see if there is a place near you where bats are likely to be roosting. Bats like somewhere sheltered, for example, a hollow tree, caves, roof spaces, eaves and soffits, behind hanging tiles, old barns and of course man-made roosts such as bat boxes.

You could try putting up a bat box in your own garden. This does require a bit of planning, though, as bats are most likely to use the box if you put it up in late winter or early spring, just before they emerge from their hibernation.

The best time to spot bats is on a clear night with a bit of moonlight. A waxing moon is a good start. You need to start your bat watch just before sunrise or sunset. Make sure you wrap up warm as the nights can get cold at this time of year, and take waterproofs, a warm drink and something to sit on. Now, all that's left to do is to find a spot near where you think the bats are roosting and wait.

Bats are small, fly fast and they can fly high, but in order to fly they need to drop 2 or 3 feet towards the ground before taking off, so you are most likely to spot a bat as it does this.

Finally, make a note in your Adventure Journal of what bats you spot and any other wildlife you discover on your watch.

Spider Web Hunt

Spiders can construct their intricate webs in under an hour, which is a good job because, just like the spider in 'If, At First, You Don't Succeed', sometimes they do not last the day before they are damaged or knocked out of the way. Yet somehow, spiders find the energy to build another.

There are approximately 650 species of spider in the UK, and they make a variety of different types of web. For this activity, we are going to see how many different types of spider's web you can find.

You will need:
* your Adventure Journal
* a pencil
* a mister – the kind you use for plants, but you can make one out of an old spray bottle. Just make sure it's well cleaned out.

How to:
Find a spot where there are plenty of places for spiders to make webs. This could be an open public space, your own garden or even your garage or shed at home.

Some webs may be easy to see, but if you can't see any at first, try spraying the mister on a hedge, bush or corner of the shed. If there is a web there, the droplets will land on the threads and you will be able to see it clearly. Make sure you just spray lightly, though, as the spiders don't mind the rain but really don't like floods.

Once you've found a web, take a closer look at it. Is it an old web? Is there a spider in it? What does the web look like? Finally, have a go at drawing the web in your Adventure Journal and see if you can identify any spiders that are in the web.

Types of web you might find:

* Orb webs – your classic spiders' webs and have threads running through them like the spokes of a wheel. The spider then weaves threads around the spokes in a circle. You may find that some species of spider decorate these webs in different ways – can you see?
* Sheet webs – you will find these strung out horizontally in the grass or hedgerows. You won't be able to see the filaments of the web clearly and they look like a bundle of spiders' silk, but to the spider they are very organised. These webs collect anything that falls into them from above or as it is passing.
* Tangle webs – exactly as their name suggests, they look like a haphazard construction. They are home to Dictynidae spiders. They are most often found on old foliage, so they are perfect for spotting at this time of year as the seasons turn.
* Funnel webs – often clearly visible on a dewy morning or a rainy day, funnel webs are found on the ground, in the grass or at the bottom of hedgerows. There will be a clear opening and then the web tapers off into the under-growth where there will be a space for the spider to hide and leap out at its prey.

There are many more types of spider webs to be found but these are some of the most common. Have fun hunting for the wondrous homes of spiders but do be careful not to damage them or the poor little spider will have to build a new one.

Pause as the Wheel Turns

Samhain

The nights draw in and it's a time of reflection and preparation for the coming winter. Samhain, or Halloween as many call it, is a time to honour the circle of life and remember those who came before us, the knowledge they have given us and the lessons we have learned from them.

It is thought that on the night of Samhain, the liminal space between this world and the next is at its thinnest. The souls of the dead walk among us and are celebrated. In some cultures, a place is set at the table for ancestors who are no longer with us, so all can share a family meal and we can say goodbye.

Samhain is an old Irish word and can be translated as 'summer's end', recognition that the abundance of the harvest has been gathered and now it is time to prepare for the winter. At the Samhain feast, bones from the meat of this year's cattle, now eaten, were thrown on the fire in the hope they will bring good luck for the herd next year.

The animals and symbols typically associated with this festival often held significance or were used as tools to predict the future. If you see a spider, it might just harbour the soul of your ancestor. Birds such as crows were counted and the direction they were flying in and the number was thought to be significant. It's also thought that if bats fly early on Samhain night then it means we are in for good weather.

Hag Stone Necklace

For centuries, folklore has told us that the hag stone is lucky and a way of divining the future. Look through the hag stone and you will see the future, carry it with you and it will bring you luck. You can find hag stones on the beach as they are commonplace and are often washed up by the tide. These stones have a hole through them and that's what makes them lucky.

I have suggested you use red wool for this craft as red is considered a lucky colour and one that is thought to represent protection, but you can use any colour you would like.

What you will need:
* red wool or cord
* a small hag stone from the beach.

To make:
First, take a trip to your local beach to find a small hag stone. Don't forget, this hag stone is going to be a necklace, so make sure it's small enough that it's not too heavy on your neck once you string it. It can be cold at this time of year, so you will want to wrap up warm and you might want to wear waterproofs and wellington boots.

(While you are at the beach you could try looking for some fossils too. Some beaches have lots of these and you can find a link to a list of good fossil-hunting beaches in the back of the book. Some of the most common fossils you will find are ammonites, belemnites, shark's teeth and sea urchins. You can find a link to more information about these in the resources at the back of the book and some pictures of them in Figure 2, again at the back of the book.)

Once you've found your hag stone and you're home again, give it a good clean and dry.

Now take the coloured cord/wool and cut three lengths so that it is long enough for you to hang around your neck after it has been plaited.

Plait the cord, then knot it well at either end. Thread your hag stone and knot each end of the plaited cord/wool together.

There, you have a necklace!

Purple Pumpkin Soup

Serves 6
This is a great way to use up pumpkin after you've carved out your Jack O' Lantern, but before we get going with the soup, there's just a little note on pumpkins. It has become increasingly popular to grow large pumpkins that are not that tasty, as there is a huge market for people buying pumpkins purely for carving at this time of year. So, when buying your pumpkin check it's a tasty variety and not one purely grown for the aesthetics and carving potential. Cinderella pumpkins look beautiful but they aren't that tasty. Here's a list of tasty types of pumpkins and squash to help you, and if you are not sure check with the person you are buying the pumpkin from:

* red kuri
* crown prince squash
* Queensland blue
* winter pumpkin
* amazonka
* hundredweight.

You could even try growing your own pumpkins from seed, but you will need to start growing them in April and check the descriptions on the seed packets to ensure they will be good for eating.

Ingredients
the flesh from one medium-sized pumpkin
500g purple carrots
600g white potatoes
1 or 2 garlic cloves, depending on your taste
2 stock cubes of your choice (beef, chicken or vegetable work best)
1 onion
2 tbsp oil
250ml milk or milk replacement (soy cream would also work well in this soup)
water

Method
* Wash, peel and cube the carrots, potato and larger pieces of pumpkin.
* Heat the oil in a large, heavy-based pan and fry the onion on a low heat until translucent. Then add the cubed vegetables. Continue to fry for a couple of minutes.
* Add the stock cubes and approximately 1 litre of water. Bring to the boil and simmer until the vegetables are soft, adding extra water if required.
* Take off the heat and cool slightly.
* Add the milk and blend. Warm the soup through and serve with thick slices of buttered bread.

November

The leaves on the trees are aflame
Red, orange, yellow and amber
The seed heads rattle in hedgerows
And the mice hide their heads in slumber

The Star Beetle

There once was a little dung beetle. He worked hard all day rolling his ball of dung. To everyone else it looked as if he was just rolling it around, but the truth was, the dung beetle longed to reach the stars – and he had a plan.

Every night he'd stop and look up at the wonderful constellations about him. Canis major, the dog, Aquila, the eagle, Ursa, the bear, and Leo, the lion. All these shapes were of fierce and magical animals, but what they really needed, thought the little dung beetle, was a beetle star. If he could just get up there to rearrange them then he would have his wish.

Every day, he rolled the dung ball and every night he got a little closer to the stars. As the months passed by, he left his friends behind; years later, the trees had disappeared and were tiny fluffs of green way below. Finally, one night he reached up and at last he could touch the stars.

As he stretched to pull the stars together in a beetle shape, he became distracted. Close by was the round, iridescent glow of the glorious full Moon. The stars didn't seem so important in her light. Perhaps if he kept on rolling the dung, he could reach her and be the first beetle on the Moon.

He rolled and rolled, spending many more years rolling the dung until, at last, the night came when he could reach the Moon herself. But the Moon did not see the beetle as she was looking at the other side of Earth.

As he reached out to touch her, she had such a shock that a blast of her cold atmosphere hit the little beetle and his ball of dung. The dung froze, shattered and cracked, disintegrating until the beetle had fallen many miles and was back on Earth once more.

Picking himself up, he looked up at the Moon. He had been so close! Not only had he not reached the Moon, but he'd also been so distracted he'd forgotten to move the stars, as he'd promised himself he would. He would never do it now. He was much too old to start again.

Shaking his wings in frustration, iridescent lights danced around him and, looking back, he saw tiny jewels of brilliant greens, dazzling blues and shining purples in his shell. Smiling, the beetle saw he had the stars on his coat and he no longer needed to look up to have his own star constellation because there it was in his jacket.

Now, every day, the dung beetle gives thanks to the stars. Using the stars above, the beetle makes a map and follows it as he rolls the dung each night and the stars always help him find the way home, because they know the little dung beetle is a star too – a little star beetle.

The Sweetest Song

In a garden owned by a man named William there is a bird that sings from the top of the old plane tree at the end of the lawn. Perched among the dappled branches, the bird sings clear and bright. His voice can be heard for miles. His singing is fresh rain on parched grass, it nourishes the soul, and all would say it is the sweetest song they have ever heard.

When the autumn came, William closed the windows against the cold north wind. He sat beside the window that looked out onto his garden and he watched the leaves fall from the old plane tree. Now he could clearly see the bird that had sung so sweetly in the summer. It still sang, but William could no longer hear it; after all, the windows were shut.

William longed to hear the sound once more, but he did not want to open the window. He would be cold. So, he decided he would like to catch the bird and bring it inside to sing for him. 'I will feed it well,' he thought to himself. 'Give it the finest food and the purest water. Surely its song will only get better.'

So, William wrapped up warm in a coat and scarf and set off down the garden to climb the plane tree and catch the bird, a little white cage, in the shape of a bell, in his hand. He climbed the tree with little trouble and the little bird did not fight him. Instead, it sat in the cage quietly and preened his colourful feathers.

William, pleased with his morning's work, took the bird inside the house and placed him in the front room. Every day, William fed the bird the finest millet and prepared him perfectly filtered water, but the bird did not sing. It was silent. Not a tweet.

Instead, the bird watched William from the cage. It preened itself, ate the millet, drank the water, but never, ever sang.

William thought perhaps the bird needed company and so he sat with him, in the front room, for hours. It was to no avail. Winter wore on, the garden outside grew bare and William felt sure the bird had a much better life inside, yet still the bird did not sing.

He thought perhaps the bird wanted some fresh air and so he put on an extra jumper and opened the window. He moved the caged bird closer to it but still it did not sing.

Finally, he decided that the bird must have forgotten how to sing, so he played it flute concertos on an old gramophone – but still it did not sing.

William sighed. 'You have such a beautiful voice, why will you not sing?'

Much to William's surprise the bird spoke. 'Because I have nothing to sing about,' it said.

'What do you mean? I give you the finest food, the purest water, company, fresh air and beautiful music. You want for nothing!'

'Ah, but I do not have my freedom,' the bird replied.

William saw the folly of his plan. He had wanted to give the bird a better life, forgetting that, perhaps, the bird already had the best life he could want. 'I am sorry,' replied William. 'I did not realise. I will set you free.'

'And in return, I will sing for you every day,' the bird replied, hope in his voice once more.

William took the cage outside to the garden and let the bird fly free. The bird soared high into the sky, bobbing and skimming along on the waves of air until he alighted in the plane tree once more and sang. He sang louder and with more harmony than he had ever sung before and when William heard it, his eyes filled with tears of joy.

Now, every day, William leaves the bird some of the finest millet and the purest water on the back doorstep. Then he sits in his garden and listens to the sweetest song.

The Proud Tree

Once there was a beech tree who stood tall in the forest. Each year, she would sprout green leaves and tiny pointed seeds surrounded by a prickly outer casing. Each autumn her leaves would fade and crinkle, the seeds would brown and both would fall from the tree.

The beech tree was proud and she didn't like to be naked in the winter, with her beautiful orange and red leaves scattered on the ground. She looked around and saw the pine tree, the holly and the silver birch, who all looked so lovely in the winter, and she wondered, 'How can I be that magnificent in the winter?'

She asked the pine tree first. 'What is your secret, pine tree?'

'I may never shed my pine needles,' replied the pine, 'but they are never the beautiful red colour that your leaves are.'

'This is true,' replied the beech. 'What about you?' she asked the holly. 'Your berries are lovely and red.'

'They are, but the birds eat them quick enough when the weather gets cold.'

'That is true, holly.' The beech tree was thoughtful. 'Silver Birch, how do you grow such wonderful bark?' she asked next.

'It is a glorious silver isn't it? But it is sought after for firelighters and I shed it easily. I cannot seem to keep it.'

'That is also true.' The beech thought hard. 'I've got it! It's simple!'

'Is it?' replied the trees together.

'Oh, yes! I shall hold on tight to my orange and red leaves. They are up high so no one can reach them like they do your bark, silver birch, and they are not tasty like your berries, holly. If I keep them until the new leaves grow then I will be beautiful all year round, and I'll never have to stand bare and dark against the sky again.'

And so that's what the beech tree does. She holds on to her flaming winter leaves until the buds of new leaves start to appear. Next time you are in the woods, take a look.

The Perfect Blend

In a village not too far from here there was a seller of tea. In his shop were tea leaves from every corner of the earth: lemon tea, rose tea, black tea, green tea, oolong, lapsang, earls and ladies; he was the man who sold it and people came from far and wide to buy it.

Despite his fortune, the tea seller was not happy. He had yet to find the perfect blend of tea leaves. One day, he turned the sign on his shop door to 'Closed'. He walked into a little room at the back of the shop and shut the door. A small window cast shimmering sun across the workbench, and he began to search the leaves for the ultimate blend. A pinch of this with a pinch of that.

Day followed night and night followed day. Many people knocked on his door, but he did not hear; he was deaf to the world in his hunt for perfection. But he grew tired, weary – exhausted, in fact – and after many moons, he fell asleep face down in the tea leaves.

He slept for hours – he did not know how long – but out of the darkness of his sleep he heard an urgent knocking. 'Let me in! Let me in! I have many people visiting my house and I need tea to welcome them.'

The tea seller awoke and wiped the grog of sleep from his eyes. The voice was honeyed and sang out. He had to see who it was. Staggering to the front door, he opened it and peered through the gap into the sunlit street. There he saw a young woman in a hessian dress, her hair in a scarf and a face full of worry.

'I need tea,' she said, holding an empty little jar out to the tea seller.

'I am sorry, I cannot sell you tea today,' he replied.

As the woman looked closer, she saw the leaves stuck to the seller's face and the emptiness in his eyes. 'Are you OK?' she asked.

'I cannot find the perfect blend,' the tea seller replied.

'But you already have it!' The woman's eyes were wide and bright.

The tea seller threw the door open. 'Come in, come in,' he hurried her inside. 'Show me, show me what it is!'

He herded his visitor through to the back room. She saw the tea leaves strewn across his workbench, and saw the turmoil, confusion and despair that lay there. 'Go and wash your face; I will make us tea,' she said, and she set about gathering the discord of leaves together.

When the tea seller returned, refreshed, the woman was seated at the table, a cup of steaming tea in front of her and a cup opposite, for him.

He sat down on the empty chair and they began to drink. They talked of love and sadness, of life and loss, of family and joy.

When he had finished his tea, the seller looked down at his empty cup and then at the woman. He saw her sparkling, smiling calm and said, 'That was a beautiful cup of tea.'

'The perfect blend,' she replied.

'You must write down the combination for me.' The seller started to move from his seat to find paper and a pen.

'There is no secret!' laughed the woman. 'Only when you drink with friends, talk of matters from the heart and share life's journey do you have the perfect blend.'

The tea seller sat back in his chair and laughed. Warmth filled his heart. His soul was mended and his mind was at peace.

Activities

Stargazing

There are millions of stars in the sky and many of them form constellations like those mentioned in the story of the 'Star Beetle'. A constellation is a group of stars that make the shape of an animal, person or object. Dung beetles really do use these groups of stars to navigate and so can we, although not so much these days with the wonders of GPS and mobile phones.

Stargazing is a great activity for all the family. Many of the constellations in the sky have stories associated with them. For this activity, you don't need special equipment, just a clear night and warm clothes.

Here are some constellations you might be able to spot and how they might look. There are some simple pictures of these star groups in Figure 3, at the back of the book:

* Ursa Major (Great Bear) – also contains the Plough within its shape
* Ursa Minor (Little Bear)
* Draco
* Orion (you may spot Orion's Belt first)
* Canis Major
* The Seven Sisters.

Don't forget to take your Adventure Journal with you so that you can record what you can see in the sky. You could even try drawing the night sky in your book. A simple way to do this would be to take a pencil and completely shade in a blank page. Then take an eraser and rub out the pencil so you have little white patches where the stars are, creating yourself a map of the sky.

Still Singing

There are many species of bird that are resident to the UK, and although they do not sing as much in the winter, you should still be able to hear them occasionally. For this activity, we are going to see how many birds you can hear in your garden. You do not need binoculars but they can be useful for checking the identification of birds if you have some that you can use. Below are six birds and their calls for you to see if you can hear them:

- robin – a sweet song, with the occasional sharp 'tic' sound. There are rarely repeated sections or pauses within its song.
- blackbird – a melodic, slightly burbling call with repeated sections of song, louder and more piercing than a robin's. Blackbirds also have a very distinct alarm call.
- long-tailed tit – a little like the noise you get if you suck your teeth. It's a trill with no whistling and often very quiet. Long-tailed tits are rarely found on their own and travel around in groups, which are easily spotted in the bare branches.
- wren – a very loud, shrill song with a trill at the end of it punctuated by three pips. This sound is usually at about knee height in the ivy on fences or in small shrubs.
- rook – these birds make a similar sound to crows as they caw, but this is generally a softer caw and they also make a range of other noises that come from their throats, which crows do not tend to do.
- magpie – very distinct in their cackling machine-gun-like call and they sound as if they are continually bickering or laughing at each other.

To listen to birds, you will need to find a spot in your garden or local green space where you can sit quietly and comfortably for a while. Make sure you are wrapped up warm and take a hot drink with you, if you would like. You could also take your Adventure Journal to make a note of what birds you hear or see.

Once you've found your spot, try and sit quietly for at least fifteen minutes and see what you can hear. It may take you a little while to tune into the bird song but it's well worth taking the time to do so. You can find out more about bird identification using the links to resources at the back of the book.

Autumn Leaf Bowl

There are so many beautiful leaves on the ground at the moment and they are perfect for crafting. For this craft, we are going to create an autumnal leaf bowl.

You will need:
- lots of freshly collected autumn leaves
- a large bowl
- cling film
- PVA glue
- paintbrush.

How To:

Take a walk in your garden, your local green space or out in the countryside and look at the different fallen leaves. You should spot, chestnut, beech, oak, sycamore and many more. Collect the different colours you find: yellow, orange, red, rust, dark brown.

At home, gently dry the leaves if they are a little damp and brush off any loose bits of dirt outside.

Take a large bowl and cover it with cling film. Place the bowl upside down with some newspaper underneath to catch any glue drips.

Spread a layer of glue on the cling film and add the leaves, gently pressing them down into the glue with the paintbrush. Cover the leaves with a second layer of glue as you add them.

Keep going until the bowl is covered with leaves and glue. Leave to dry overnight.

You can add a second layer of leaves at this point if you like and leave it to dry again.

Finally, when the layers are completely dry, lift the cling film off the bowl and gently pull it from the leaves. You should now have an autumn leaf bowl.

Apple and Marigold Tea

Makes a 500ml jar

You too can become a maker of tea and find your perfect blend, like the tea seller in 'The Perfect Blend'. For this activity, we are going to make a magical apple and marigold tea.

You can buy the ingredients for this tea in a good wholefood store or herbalists. You could forage and dry your own herbs for this recipe, but you must make absolutely sure you know what you are picking. The first rule of foraging is – do not eat or drink anything you are not sure of.

At the end of the recipe, I have included how to dry your own apples if you would like to try this out.

Ingredients

25g dried nettles
25g dried marigolds
3 cinnamon sticks
1 apple (dried)

Method

Add the dried nettles and marigolds to the jar. Crush the cinnamon sticks up and add them. Cut the dried apple rings into chunks and add those. Mix thoroughly and keep the jar in a cool, dry kitchen cupboard. Use to your taste but 2–3 tsp for a large teapot, brewed for at least 5 minutes, is recommended.

How to dry apples

Peel and core one apple. Slice into rings and lay on a baking tray. Cook in a fan oven on the lowest setting, approximately 80°C, for one and a half to two hours.

December

Tree skeletons hang heavy with snow
Icicles drip in the morning the sun
This month holds the darkest days
As we wait for spring to come.

Arne

Arne was born a Viking. He watched the warriors from his basket as he was rocked to the singing of his mother, songs of great conquest and bravery. As Arne grew, he learned of the Viking ways, the way of the warrior and the path to Valhalla.

To the warriors of the clan, fighting and death in battle was an honour embraced by all. To Arne, fighting and conquests only brought with them violence and tears. Not everyone returned. Arne saw that they had plenty in their village. They had no need for more land, slaves or food for their tables. They had what they needed and so, for Arne, fighting was not always necessary.

Arne grew older still and as a young boy, he learnt to ice skate using the carved bones of animals, strapped to his shoes. It was an important skill for any Viking living in a land where there was lots of ice. It helped them to travel from place to place in the winter. But Arne didn't just skate to get across the frozen lands – he skated for the joy and for the pleasure, for the way the wind felt on his face and for the exhilarating speed at which he could travel. His cheeks were always rosy, and his eyes always sparkled. Many of his friends skated with him, learning to navigate the frozen lands, but none skated for the pure joy of it, as Arne did.

As he grew into a young man, his father no longer tolerated Arne skating just for the fun of it. He wanted Arne to complete his training to become a warrior. He wanted him to come with him on raids with the other Viking warriors. But Arne was adamant he would not. And so as far as Arne's father was concerned, Arne had disgraced his family.

Arne's mother begged him to make peace with his father. Arne tried. His love for his parents drove him to find compromise and so Arne learned to use a broadsword and he did this while he skated across the ice. And so it was that Arne learnt to move faster than any warrior ever could.

But Arne still believed fighting should only be as a last resort and could not embrace the warrior tradition. When Arne continued to refuse to go with them on raids, his father refused to acknowledge him as a warrior.

The day came when Arne's father was away from the village, as well as many other warriors. It was one of the coldest winters they had ever seen, and the long boats were having trouble returning home in the cold and frozen seas.

A call went out from the village lookout that a ship had arrived. It was not their own. Its heavily armed crew had reached land and were now moving across the frozen fjord towards the village. The clan was in turmoil, running to secure livestock and putting out fires so they could not be used to set light to their houses. Finally, the children were taken to safety in the Long Hall.

Arne took up his sword. Now was his chance to shine. The ice was thick on the fjord and he knew it like the back of his hand. Gathering a few of the villagers together, he explained his plan. Taking their skates and weapons, they headed to the frozen fjord, where they strapped the bone skates to their feet and set off. Being careful to stay out of sight, Arne directed them to various points along the fjord. Then skating in a triangular formation, they moved in behind the armed strangers.

With an almighty cry, Arne led the group forward and skated as he had never skated before. The marauding strangers were so shocked that they stumbled as they reached for their swords. Arne beat down one after another like skittles and, as they turned and moved backwards in the direction in which Arne now herded them, the ice started to crack. You see, the fjord ice was thick in most places but not in every place, and Arne knew just where it was at its weakest. The vanquished warriors disappeared beneath the ice and were never seen again. No longer a threat to Arne's village.

From that day forward, Arne was hailed a hero. His father often asks him to tell the tale in the Long Hall around the fire and now Arne teaches the younger members of the village to be great ice warriors, just as he is.

George, the Noisy Gander

George arrived in the spring and immediately broke the peace of the farmyard with his bossy ways. 'Don't walk there … Get off my land … That's my food … Move out of my way!' He wasn't just bossy, he was noisy, unpleasant and annoying. The other geese were fed up.

The year had worn on and now it was December. Snow had fallen on the ground. George wanted the other geese to move it out of the way so he could reach the food trough without walking through the cold snow.

'You're only good for bossing people around!' said a plucky goose named Giselle.

'Out of my way or get digging,' George replied. 'I'm very important, don't you know. I get the best food because I make the biggest noise.'

'Biggest amount of hot air you mean!' Giselle huffed, and walked into the goose shed to warm up. She fluffed out her feathers and listened to the kerfuffle in the yard as George bossed the other geese around. It was then that she heard it – the far-off sound of singing. She'd heard it before and knew they were called carols. It was Christmas.

Giselle had seen several Christmases. She knew she was only still around because of her good nature and reliable eggs. She was grateful for that. She huddled back onto her shelf-shaped bed and waited. It was the same every year. Christmas meant only one thing – one goose fewer in the farmyard and one goose on the table for dinner.

She was awoken from her doze by George's shrill voice. 'See, they want me to go with them now; they have even better food inside. I've seen it.'

Giselle rushed outside. 'Don't follow them, George. It's a trick. It's Christmas!'

'I know and they want me to share their dinner with them. See how important I am.'

'No …' Giselle tried again.

'Shh! Giselle, you're just jealous,' George shouted over his shoulder as he headed towards the outbuildings attached to the farm.

From that day on, the farm was a much quieter place to be. Now Giselle tells the story of the noisy arrogant goose to the little goslings in the nursery as a reminder to be kind to each other and never trust the humans at Christmas.

Every Horse Has Her Day

This is the story of a carousel horse called Edith.

Edith had been riding on the fair circuit for about twenty years. She loved the bright lights, the tinny music and the squeals of delight as the children bobbed up and down, but there was one thing that Edith longed for.

Each horse had the same wooden saddle, the same gold, twisted pole for the rider to hold, the same battered leather reins and the same red mane. The only difference between them was a circle on their flanks with a gold number in it.

Charlie, the horse in front of her, was number one. That meant Edith was number two. No matter how hard she galloped, no matter how many leaps and bounds she made, no matter how many children chose to ride her instead of Charlie, she was always number two.

'I wish I could be number one, Charlie,' Edith said.

'We are fixed,' Charlie replied. 'We can only move up and down, Edith.'

'I know, but I do so wish I could be up at the front.'

'Even if you were,' Charlie replied, 'you'd still be behind someone. We're all behind someone.'

The fair continued to travel around the country and Edith galloped along listening to the screeches of unfettered joy, smelling the hot sugar candyfloss, feeling the small hands grip her mane. It was a good life, but for Edith it was not quite good enough.

As time moved on, the paint on her saddle became chipped, Edith's legs became warped, and the hairs of her tail moulted away. All eight horses were a sorry sight and the fairground owner decided to retire them. The carousel was sold to a scrapyard and there the horses were taken apart, falling broken, tired and unloved on the rubbish heap.

Edith longed for the fair ground days when the children had ridden her. Lying in the dirt among the shattered mirrors, pieces of kitchen sink and defunct washing machines, Edith realised that second place had been heaven compared to this.

'I'm sorry I complained so much, Charlie,' she sighed.

'Don't give up hope, Edith. Someone will find us,' Charlie replied.

'But who?'

Day followed night and winter came. Charlie had gone to another home, along with several of the other carousel horses and Edith was lonely. The skies were clear and cold, and she looked up at the stars as snow began to fall. One morning, cold to her very last splinter, Edith heard a voice.

'That one, mummy.'

'Are you sure? It's very old.'

'Yes!' said the little girl as she walked up to where Edith lay and pushed the snow from her nose. 'This one.'

Edith felt the warmth of the little girl's hands as she lifted her into a dark box and closed the lid; whoomp! The whole thing began to move and eventually, after some time in the dark, whatever it was she was in stopped. Sunlight flooded the box again. Edith was carried to a small shed and the little girl's mother began her work.

She sanded Edith down, removing all her paint. The leatherwork on her reins was re-stitched and the stirrups of the saddle were replaced. Then the girl's mother carved out two bent pieces of wood and attached them to Edith's feet. Finally, she replaced her mane with glittery white hair and polished her nose until it shone.

'There,' she said. 'And a fine rocking horse you make too.'

When the little girl saw Edith, she could not contain her excitement. She leapt into the saddle and spent the afternoon rocking backwards and forwards, stroking Edith's mane and only leaving Edith when she was called to dinner.

Edith looked at her side. There was no number anymore, just shiny, varnished wood. Edith sighed. At last she could see that she didn't need to be number one to bring laughter to children and find joy herself.

The Dog and the Giant

There once was a dog who lived with a man who didn't treat him well. He didn't treat him well at all. The man kept the dog to chase away the rats and only fed him on scraps of dried bread and bacon rind. The dog's tummy grumbled continually. If the dog begged for more food, he was kicked. It was not a happy life.

One day the dog smelt the familiar smell of sausages, but it wasn't coming from the stove as it usually did. Sticking his head outside the door, he saw a huge sausage just lying in the middle of the road that ran alongside the house. He sniffed the air and the sausage smelt good. Trotting up to it the dog gave it a lick. It tasted good too.

'Don't eat that!' tweeted a bird from high up in the old oak tree.

'But I'm so hungry,' replied the dog.

'It belongs to the grumpy giant who lives in the castle over there,' the bird pointed with its wing. 'He dropped it on his way home from the market and he won't be pleased.'

But the dog was so hungry, he couldn't help himself and ate the sausage in three bites – one, two, three. When he was done, he could still smell sausage.

Following the smell, he walked further along the road and saw another sausage.

'Don't eat that!' bleated the sheep in the field.

'But I'm so hungry,' replied the dog.

'It belongs to the grumpy giant who lives in the castle over there,' the sheep pointed with its hoof. 'He dropped it on his way home from the market and he won't be pleased.'

But the dog was so hungry, he couldn't help himself and ate the sausage in three bites – one, two three. When he was done, he could still smell sausage.

Walking on further, he saw another sausage. He couldn't believe his luck and bounded up to it.

'Don't eat that!' said the horse, walking along the road back towards town.

'But I'm so hungry,' replied the dog.

'It belongs to the grumpy giant who lives in the castle over there,' the horse pointed with its nose. 'He dropped it on his way home from the market and he won't be pleased.'

But the dog was so hungry, he couldn't help himself and ate the sausage in three bites – one, two, three. When he was done, he could still smell sausage.

The dog walked on and found another and another, followed by another. Each time someone warned him not to eat it, but he couldn't help himself and ate until his stomach was round and tight.

Eventually he arrived at the giant's castle. The sausages had led him there and now he was so full and so tired he fell asleep on the doorstep.

After a while, a booming voice woke the dog. 'You've eaten all my sausages!' It was the giant, and he was so cross that the bowler hat he was wearing was shaking.

'I'm so sorry,' whimpered the dog. 'I was sooo hungry. I didn't mean to make you more grumpy.'

'What do you mean grumpy?' frowned the giant.

'Everyone says you're grumpy.'

The giant looked sad. 'I'm not grumpy, little dog. I'm lonely.'

The dog jumped up, wagging his tail with hope. 'I'll be your friend!' smiled the dog. 'I would love to live here with you and eat more of those wonderful sausages!'

'Then you shall,' replied the giant. And from that day forth, the dog was never hungry and the giant was never lonely; they were firm friends for the rest of their lives.

Activities

Go Ice Skating

Ice skating is a very popular activity at this time of year and we've been taking part in this sport for over 1,000 years.

According to the *Encyclopaedia Britannica*, it is thought that ice skating originated in Scandinavia around 1000 BCE. The first skates would have been made from animal bones that were strapped to the wearer's feet. The little Viking in our story 'Arne' would have had skates made of horse or cattle bones. They may have been polished on one side and a hole drilled into them through which a leather thong was threaded so that they could be tied to his feet. You can see an example of these skates in the Jorvik Viking Centre in York, as several pairs were discovered by archaeologists in a group of finds at a place called 'Coppergate'. You can find a link to more information and pictures of this find in the back of the book.

It wasn't until the 1800s that the metal blades we know were developed and attached to a piece of wood that fitted under the wearer's shoe. And then it wasn't until much later, when skating became a competitive sport, that the blades became much lighter and more engineered.

Throughout the seventeenth century, skating outside on frozen ponds, rivers and even the marshy fens was very popular and during this time, known as 'The Little Ice Age', the River Thames would occasionally freeze, allowing people to skate on it in what were known as 'Frost Fairs'.

In our current climate, skating on frozen ponds or rivers is definitely not recommended and is extremely dangerous, as we saw in the story of Arne the Viking. The ice will not hold a person's weight and you may end up under the ice. However, these days there are often pop-up rinks in towns and cities that you can visit. Your local sports centre may have one too. You will be able to hire skates there and try out skating for yourself. Don't forget to take your Adventure Journal and write down what it felt like to skate like a Viking.

Taking a Gander

Geese aren't just found on the farm, like 'George, the Noisy Gander'. Many of our winter bird visitors in the UK are geese and for this activity we are going to take a gander at geese. To do this, you will need warm clothes, binoculars if you have them, your Adventure Journal and a pen or pencil.

First, you will need to find a place to go to spot the geese. This can be a nature reserve, or an inlet of water or harbour that you can get to via marked footpaths. The Wildfowl & Wetlands Trust is a good place to start and there is a link to a list of the reserves in the back of this book. If you decide to go geese spotting beside the shore, be careful that you are not standing on a spit of land that will be cut off when the tide comes in.

Once you've found a good goose-spotting area, you can find somewhere to sit or stand and watch the wildfowl. You may find that if you are in a reserve there are information boards telling you what birds you might be able to see but here are five geese you might spot at this time of year:

- brent goose – the brent goose is a small goose with a black head and white ring around its neck. It has a black beak, black legs and a white rump. It is a very noisy goose, so you may hear it before you see it.
- Canada goose – the Canada goose is a very well-known goose and again has a black head and beak. This goose has a white chin and a white rump but has lighter, more brown feathers than the brent goose.
- pink-footed goose – the pink-footed goose is so called because of its pink feet. This makes it an easy one to spot. You may also see a small pink mark on its otherwise black beak. The colouring on the rest of this goose is a mottled brown-black colour, darker than the greylag goose.
- greylag goose – the greylag goose also has pink legs, but this goose has a completely pink bill. It's body shape means it looks more like your standard picture book goose. It is grey-brown in colour.
- Egyptian goose – Egyptian geese are very colourful geese. They have pink-black beaks with a black ring around their eye. Their pinion feathers are brown, rust and a turquoise blue in colour and their legs are bright pink. They are smaller than a greylag or pink-footed goose and are very distinctive.

Pause as the Wheel Turns

Yule

As the holly berries grow fat and the nights draw closer, the battle between the light and the dark is almost over for another year. The wheel turns and the frost sets the ground, arresting nature, pressing pause and turning in.

The winter solstice falls between 20 and 23 December. It is generally accepted that the 21st is Yule, the celebration of the longest night and the return of the light. For the Anglo-Saxons, December was called *Aerra Giul* – 'before Yule' – and Yule is one of the most well-known sabbats within the wheel of the year.

With the colourful leaves and petals of summer gone, the world seems a little less full, but there is still time to gather pine cones, holly, mistletoe and fir branches to decorate the home and hearth. Some take an almost completely burnt log from last year's fire and use it to start the Yule fire on the 21st. This is the tradition known as the Yule log and again is a reminder of the cycle of life.

The house is filled with the smells of home baking, cedar, juniper, pine, cinnamon and frankincense. It is a time for rest and reflection. A time to spend curled up by the fire, with no rushing allowed. This is our time for rebirth.

Jam Jar Candleholder

At this time of year, many of us decorate the house for Christmas and Yuletide, so it's a great time to get creative with Christmas decorations. Like the mother in 'Every Horse Has Her Day', we are going to do a bit of upcycling for this activity and make a simple jam jar candleholder.

You will need:
- clean, empty jam jar
- baking parchment
- scissors
- string or sticky tape
- tealights.

How to make:

Cut out a piece of the baking parchment that will fit around the circumference of your jar and is wide enough to cover most of the sides of the jar.

Draw the outlines of stars, moon, holly leaves or whatever pattern you would like onto the paper. Using scissors, cut out the shapes you have made in the baking paper so that you now have different shaped holes in your paper. The paper should still be in one long piece, like a stencil.

Wrap the paper around the jar and tie it in place at the top and the bottom with string or secure it with a bit of sticky tape.

Place the tea light in the jar and carefully light. The light should flicker through the shapes in the paper and if you turn your electric lights out on a dark evening, you should be able to project little shapes of light onto the walls so that they decorate the whole house.

Pigs in Blankets and Yorkshire Puddings

You could try making this one together to go with your Christmas dinner or have it as a meal on its own served with peas and gravy. If you are going to have this dish as a main meal, you may want to use eight sausages instead of four.

Serves 4

Ingredients
4 large sausages
4 slices of streaky bacon
100g plain flour
pinch of salt
1 egg
150ml milk
sunflower or vegetable oil

Method
❋ You will need a large four-cup Yorkshire pudding tin for this recipe.
❋ Preheat your oven to 180°C.
❋ Sift the flour and salt into a large mixing bowl.

✳ In a separate jug, add the egg to the milk and beat well. Make a well in the middle of the flour and gradually combine the flour with the milk and egg. Do this as slowly as possible to avoid lumpy Yorkshires.

✳ Wrap one piece of streaky bacon around each sausage and place in a shallow baking dish. Place the sausages in the oven and cook for 20–25 minutes.

✳ Put a small amount of oil in the bottom of each of the cups in the Yorkshire pudding tin. Place the tin with the oil in the oven for 5 minutes. Ask an adult to remove the tray from the oven once the oil has heated up.

✳ Divide the batter between the four cups in the hot tray. Cook in the oven for a further 15–20 minutes until the puddings are golden brown.

✳ Remove the sausages and Yorkshire puddings from the oven once they are cooked. Place a sausage in each Yorkshire pudding and serve as a side dish on Christmas Day.

Resources

Below is a list of resources for each month within the book, which you can use to find more information and to help you with the activities for that month, should you wish. Don't forget, you can visit and support your local library where there are lots of books and resources, as well as access to the internet. Take this list with you and your local librarian will be happy to help you.

January

Websites

A–Z of trees: www.woodlandtrust.org.uk/trees-woods-and-wildlife/
    british-trees/a-z-of-british-trees
Find your local woodland: www.woodlandtrust.org.uk/visiting-woods/find-woods
RSPB Online Interactive Bird Identifier: www.rspb.org.uk/birds-and-wildlife/
    wildlife-guides/identify-a-bird

Books

Collins Complete British Birds by Paul Sterry
Collins Complete British Insects by Michael Chinery
Collins Complete British Animals by Paul Sterry

February

Websites

The Countryside Code: www.gov.uk/government/publications/the-countryside-code
Bee identification: www.friendsoftheearth.uk/bees/bee-identification-guide
More information on Bumblebee conservation: www.bumblebeeconservation.org

Books

Bloomsbury Pocket Guide to Wild Flowers by Bob Gibbons

March

Websites

Pond Dipping Guide: www.rspb.org.uk/fun-and-learning/for-families/
    family-wild-challenge/activities/pond-dipping
Moth identification: www.butterfly-conservation.org/moths
Moth indentification: www.ukmoths.org.uk/thumbnails/sphingidae

Books

Bloomsbury Concise Pond Wildlife Guide
Collins Complete British Insects by Michael Chinery
Bloomsbury Concise Guide to the Moths of Great Britain & Ireland by Martin Townsend
    et al

April

Websites

Guide to the weather and clouds: www.beta.metoffice.gov.uk/weather/learn-about/
    weather/types-of-weather/clouds/cloud-spotting-guide

May

Websites

Moons phases: https:www.timeanddate.com/moon/phases

June

Websites

Identifying swifts, swallows and house martins: www.community.rspb.org.uk/
    ourwork/b/rspb-england/posts/swift-swallow-or-house-martin-which-is-it-what-s-
    the-difference-and-how-can-you-tell
Stonehenge and the Solstice: www.english-heritage.org.uk/visit/places/stonehenge/
    things-to-do/stone-circle/celestial-stonehenge

More about the hummingbird hawkmoth: www.rspb.org.uk/birds-
    and-wildlife/wildlife-guides/birdwatching/how-to-identify-birds/
    hummingbirds-and-hawkmoths

Books

Collins Complete British Birds by Paul Sterry

July

Websites

Natural History Museum's guide to rock pooling: www.nhm.ac.uk/discover/how-to-go-rockpooling.html

BBC tide times: www.bbc.co.uk/weather/coast-and-sea/tide-tables

Books

RSPB First Book of the Sea Shore by Derek Niemann

August

Websites

Guide to seasonal fruit and vegetables: www.countrysideonline.co.uk/back-british-farming/cook-and-eat/a-seasonal-guide-to-british-fruit-and-vegetables

Bug hunt: www.buglife.org.uk/bugs/bug-directory

Books

Collins Complete British Insects by Michael Chinery

September

Websites

More information on geocaching: www.geocaching.com

October

Websites

Bat Conservation Trust: www.bats.org.uk

Moon phases: www.timeanddate.com/moon/phases/uk/greenwich-city

Spiders' webs: www.nhm.ac.uk/discover/spider-webs.html
Good beaches for fossil hunting: www.portalstothepast.co.uk/
    the-best-fossil-finding-beaches-in-the-uk
Common fossils: www.nationaltrust.org.uk/features/commonly-found-fossils

November

Websites

Birdsong identification: www.rspb.org.uk/birds-and-wildlife/wildlife-guides/bird-a-z/
    robin
National Geographic stargazing information: www.nationalgeographic.co.uk/
    space/2020/04/need-newidea-keep-kids-entertained-try-stargazing

Books

Bird Watching With Your Eyes Closed by Simon Barnes
National Trust Out and About Night Explorer

December

Websites

History of ice skating: www.britannica.com/sports/ice-skating
Viking ice skate: www.jorvikvikingcentre.co.uk/about/jorvik-artefact-gallery
Wildfowl and Wetlands Trust reserves: www.wwt.org.uk/wetland-centres

Books

Collins Complete Guide to British Birds by Paul Sterry

Bibliography and Further Reading

Barnes, Simon, *Bird Watching with your Eyes Closed: an Introduction to Birdsong* (Short Books, 2011).

Barnes, Simon, *Rewild Yourself: 23 Spellbinding Ways to Make Nature More Visible* (Simon & Schuster, 2018).

Bloomsbury Concise Pond Wildlife Guide (Bloomsbury, 2015).

Chamberlain, Lisa, *Wicca: Wheel of the Year Magic* (Wicca Shorts, 2017).

Chinery, Michael, *Collins Complete Guide to British Insects* (Harper Collins, 2005).

Keable, Georgiana, *The Natural Storyteller: Wildlife Tales for Telling* (Hawthorn Press, 2017).

Leendertz, Lia, *The Almanac: A Seasonal Guide to 2020* (Octopus Books, 2019).

National Trust, *Out & About Night Explorer* (Nosy Crow, 2019).

Smith, Keri, *How to be an Explorer of the World: Portable Life Museum* (Penguin, 2008).

Sterry, Paul, *Collins Complete Guide to British Birds* (Harper Collins, 2004).

Wohlleben, Peter, *The Hidden Life of Trees* (William Collins, 2016).

Worroll, Jane and Peter Houghton, *Play the Forest School Way* (Watkins Publishing, 2016).

Appendices

Fig 1:

Shark's Teeth

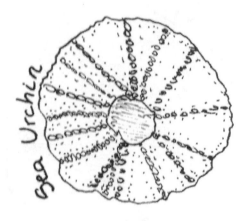

Sea Urchin

Ammonite

Belemnites

Fig 2:

Fig 3:

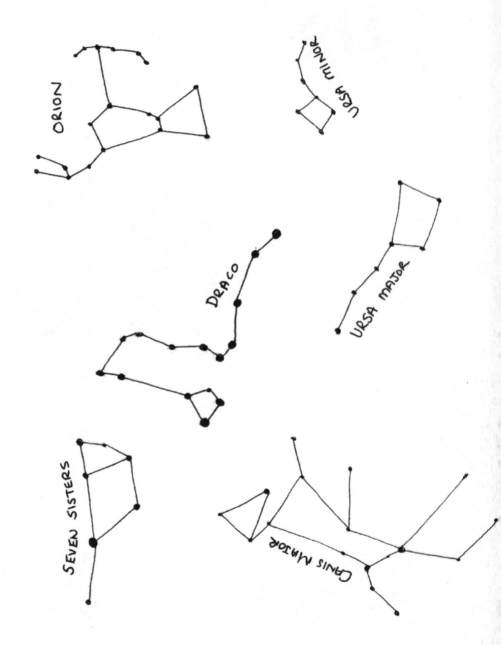